An Awareness
of What
is Missing

An Awareness of What is Missing

Faith and Reason in a Post-Secular Age

JÜRGEN HABERMAS
et al.

Translated by
CIARAN CRONIN

polity

First published in German as *Ein Bewußtsein von dem, was fehlt* ©
Suhrkamp Verlag Frankfurt am Main 2008

Polity Press
65 Bridge Street
Cambridge CB2 1UR, UK

Polity Press
350 Main Street
Malden, MA 02148, USA

ISBN-13: 978-0-7456-4720-3 (hardback)
ISBN-13: 978-0-7456-4721-0 (paperback)

A catalogue record for this book is available from the British Library.

Typeset in 11 on 13 pt Berling
by Toppan Best-set Premedia Limited
Printed and bound in Great Britain by MPG Books Group Ltd,
Bodmin, Cornwall

The publisher has used its best endeavors to ensure that the URLs
for external websites referred to in this book are correct and active
at the time of going to press. However, the publisher has no
responsibility for the websites and can make no guarantee that a site
will remain live or that the content is or will remain appropriate.

For further information on Polity, visit our website:
www.politybooks.com

The translation of this work was supported by a grant from the
Goethe-Institut which is funded by the German Ministry of Foreign
Affairs.

Contents

Contributors

NORBERT BRIESKORN, S. J. is Professor of Social and Legal Philosophy at the Jesuit School for Philosophy in Munich and is a member of its Institute for Social Policy.

JÜRGEN HABERMAS is Emeritus Professor of Philosophy at Frankfurt University.

MICHAEL REDER is Adjunct Professor of Social Philosophy and Philosophy of Religion at the Jesuit School for Philosophy in Munich and is a member of its Institute for Social Policy.

FRIEDO RICKEN, S. J. is Emeritus Professor of the History of Philosophy and Ethics at the Jesuit School for Philosophy in Munich.

JOSEF SCHMIDT, S. J. is Professor of Philosophical Theology and the History of Philosophy at the Jesuit School for Philosophy in Munich and Director of its Institute for the Philosophy of Religion.

Preface

What is meant when contemporary society is described as "post-secular"? With this concept, Jürgen Habermas has exercised a major influence on the recent debate concerning the social role and importance of religion. This is clearly testified by the widespread public response to his speech on receiving the Peace Prize of the German Book Trade in 2001, and the discussion with the then Cardinal Ratzinger at the Catholic Academy in Munich in 2004. At the center of Habermas's reflections on this issue are the questions of the relation between faith and reason and of the relation between secular and religious citizens. He challenges reason to reflect on what it is missing and on its relation to religion.

The contributors to this volume take up Habermas's challenge to reflect on "the awareness of what is missing." Their remarks are intended as contributions to the conversation with the philosopher and they wish to provide encouragement to continue the debate. The texts originated in a podium discussion between Habermas and the representatives of the Jesuit School for Philosophy – Norbert Brieskorn, Michael Reder, Friedo Ricken, and Josef Schmidt – which took place in Munich in February

2007. Habermas's contribution was followed by a lively and stimulating debate. For this volume, the participants have developed their reflections further in their contributions, into which arguments from the plenary discussion on that occasion have also found their way.

October 2007

1
Habermas and Religion

MICHAEL REDER AND JOSEF SCHMIDT, S. J.

Starting Point: The Renewed Visibility of Religion

Religion is once more a topic of debate. It is once again being increasingly perceived as a social phenomenon, a development not prompted solely by the events of September 11, 2001. Against the background of the sociological debate on secularization of the 1970s and 1980s, in western countries religions seemed destined to lose ever more of their importance with progressive modernization and individualization. Yet this hypothesis has not been confirmed; on the contrary, today religions play an extremely important role in western societies.

The social traces of religions are to be found primarily in two domains. On the one hand, they take positions on political questions or engage in public debates. This phenomenon has undoubtedly been reinforced in Germany by the fact that Pope Benedict XVI has drawn renewed attention to the Christian Churches. However, the many other religious communities – be they Islamic, Buddhist, or Hindu – are also becoming increasingly important actors within western civil societies.

On the other hand, religion in these countries has undergone a multifaceted transformation, for religious symbols and language games are being transposed into other, not genuinely religious, domains. Unmistakable borrowings from religious traditions can be found in film, theater, and advertisement and in how mass events are

1

orchestrated. In the process, the semantic and symbolic potentials of religions are becoming a universal social resource which shapes public and cultural life in a whole variety of ways.

The social significance of religion is becoming even more clearly apparent from a global perspective, for today religious communities play an important public role in very many regions of the world. They shape the individual practical attitudes of human beings in a variety of cultural ways, they influence cultural life, and they are part of public discourses and political processes. As a result, religions represent an important factor which merits attention when analyzing social developments in many parts of the world. Religion has also become a central topic on the global political stage, especially since September 11, 2001. Today global political strategies are difficult to conceive without reference to the relation between religion and politics.

Thus the discourse concerning secularization has also undergone a pronounced change. In spite of enduring trends towards secularization in certain regions (for instance, in eastern Germany), today almost nobody speaks of an imminent "extinction" of religions or of the religious any longer. Common sense seems to dictate that, although religions have changed profoundly and have been in part transformed during the modern and postmodern eras, they nevertheless remain a phenomenon of major social importance – in particular as regards the global situation. Thus "the return of the gods" – to quote the title of a book by Friedrich Wilhelm Graf (Graf 2004) – is not strictly speaking a "return"; what we are witnessing is rather a renewed attention to the religious, even if the latter today appears in a new garb.

Philosophy, too, has dealt with this phenomenon extensively in recent years. One need only think of the conference which took place on the island of Capri in 1994, in which Jacques Derrida, Gianni Vattimo, and Hans-Georg Gadamer participated, among others (Derrida and Vattimo 1998). The volume *The Future of Religion* edited by Richard Rorty and Gianni Vattimo in 2006 is a further expression of this revived interest (Rorty and Vattimo 2006).

The philosophical discourse on religion in the context of the twenty-first century is multifarious and reflects clearly the different philosophical approaches of the respective authors. Notwithstanding all differences, however, one generally encounters three major sets of shared questions: (1) What does secularization involve and how should we understand its most recent development? (2) The second complex of questions concerns the difficulty involved in describing religion itself given the initial conditions outlined. Immanuel Kant, the paradigmatic authority figure of the modern era, is repeatedly invoked in this context in connection with the question of how religion should be conceived in philosophical terms. How, for example, should the relation between faith and knowledge be conceptualized and what is the specific domain of the philosophy of religion in the light of the emergence of an interreligious reality as globalization progresses? (3) The third line of enquiry connects the two previous ones in a certain way. For many studies deal with the issue of how, in the light of the current social developments, the relation between the secular and the religious language games, between citizens and institutions, can be conceived. Do they stand in a complementary relation or must we assume a priority of the one over the other for political and ethical reasons? And, finally: What potential do religious language games and symbols have for secular citizens?

Habermas and Religion – A Relation with Many Facets

Over the past forty years, Jürgen Habermas has consistently responded creatively to political and social

3

developments. Scarcely any other philosopher has taken such an active part in current debates or has played a comparable role in initiating them. As a thinker concerned with "society as a whole," he has consistently adopted an interdisciplinary approach and has exercised a profound influence on the public life of the Federal Republic of Germany. Thus it is not surprising that he has addressed the new visibility of religion in a very stimulating way.

If one surveys Habermas's work as a whole, the first thing one notices is that, until the middle of the 1990s, it contained just a few systematic treatments of religion; nevertheless, he expressed himself at least indirectly on religion in a number of works. In what follows, we will first mention these references briefly.[1]

In *Theorie des kommunikativen Handelns* (1981; English translation: *The Theory of Communicative Action*, 1984 (vol. 1), 1987 (vol. 2)), the work in which he laid the foundation of his approach to sociology and ethics, one can find a few preliminary references to the social role of religion that are still clearly influenced by the secularization hypothesis. Habermas assumes that, with the development of modern democratic society, the function of religion in fostering social integration is essentially transferred to secularized communicative reason: ". . . the socially integrative and expressive functions that were at first fulfilled by ritual practice pass over to communicative action; the authority of the holy is gradually replaced by the authority of an achieved consensus" (Habermas 1987, p. 77). Underlying this assessment is the basic idea of communicative action, which states that communicatively acting persons reach agreements concerning their normative validity claims through rational argument and "only those norms can claim to be valid that meet (or could meet) with the approval of all affected in their capacity as participants in a practical discourse" (Habermas 1991a,

---

[1] For an overview of Habermas's "early statements" on religion, see Arens (ed.) 1989, pp. 11–17.

4

p. 93). Religion is in danger of blocking precisely this communicative action because it does not leave the religious participants in discourse free to enter the presuppositionless space of rational communication, but instead equips them with clear directives concerning the goal of the discourse. Hence Habermas calls on the religious citizens not to absolutize their one-sided (moral) judgments but instead to submit to the conditions of a liberal state. From the perspective of the theory of communicative action, religion ultimately appears to belong to a historical developmental phase along the path to the modern, democratically constituted society.

In contrast to this more religion-skeptical point of view, during the 1970s and 1980s one can already find scattered remarks which are less informed by the thrust of the secularization hypothesis and which attach greater importance to the fact that modern societies – assuming that they want to strengthen the human [*das Humane*] – depend inherently on an understanding and a translation of the potentials of religious traditions. On the occasion of Gershom Scholem's eightieth birthday, Habermas expressed this insight as follows in his interpretation of a selection of Scholem's assertions: "Among the modern societies, only those that are able to introduce into the secular domain the essential contents of their religious traditions which point beyond the merely human realm will also be able to rescue the substance of the human" (Habermas 1978, p. 142).

Ten years later, in the essays on *Postmetaphysical Thinking*, this recognition of the importance of the religious for modern societies found still clearer, if only indirect, expression. For Habermas now stresses the need to reflect on the religious if we are to be able, for example, to understand the central concepts of the history of ideas, which in many cases developed out of religious convictions. In addition to this historical knowledge, however, he emphasizes that religions contain indispensable semantic elements which differ fundamentally from philosophy and which may be

5

important for the just ordering of modern societies. However, the basic idea of the theory of communicative action is preserved in these reflections. For the analysis of postmetaphysical thinking shows that, although religion exercises an important function in dealing with meta-physical issues, it can no longer raise, any more than can philosophy, a claim to universalizability for this function; nor can it claim to perform any of the integrative functions of worldviews.

From the mid-1990s onwards, Habermas has addressed the topic of religion explicitly and has enquired, in particular, into the relation between religion and the basic assumptions of his own social theory and ethics.[2] He first addressed the question of religion in his acceptance speech on receiving the Karl Jaspers Prize in 1985. However, his speech on receiving the Peace Prize of the German Book Trade in 2001, and the discussion with the then Cardinal Ratzinger at the Catholic Academy in Munich in 2004, have attracted particular attention.

In the Peace Prize speech, entitled "Faith and Knowl-edge" (Habermas 2003), Habermas develops the idea that the secularization hypothesis has now lost its explanatory power and that religion and the secular world always stand in a reciprocal relation. Although faith and knowledge are clearly separate from one another, they inherently depend on a constructive coexistence, especially in addressing urgent social questions such as those posed by bioethics. Religion proves to be an important moral resource in this context, according to Habermas, because religious citizens have special access to a potential for justifying moral ques-tions. Its meaning-endowing function provides a moral basis for public discourse and thereby plays an important role in the public sphere.

In the light of the terrorist attacks of September 11, 2001, in particular, Habermas thinks that it is important

[2] For an outline of recent developments in Habermas's interpretation of religion, see Maly 2005.

6

to emphasize that religious expressions should not be crowded out of public discourse. On the contrary, he insists on the need to translate the contents of religious language into a secular one and thus to make them accessible to all. In this context, the concept "post-secular" – which in the interim has exerted a major influence on the debate over the social role of religion – expresses the fact that modern societies should also expect that religions will continue to exist and should seek to engage them in a constructive dialogue.

This relation of mutual dependence between faith and knowledge, between religious and secular citizens, becomes even clearer in the conversation with Cardinal Ratzinger conducted at the Catholic Academy in Munich in 2004. In addressing Ernst-Wolfgang Böckenförde's question concerning the normative presuppositions of the secularized state, Habermas stresses, on the one hand, the importance of fair and just procedures and, on the other, the fact that democratic majority decisions always depend on the prior ethical convictions of their citizens. Democracy depends on moral stances which stem from prepolitical sources, for example from religious ways of life. They play an important role for democracy as a background and a source of motivation, even though they cannot serve as normative guidelines for the democratic procedures.

However, religious utterances take on a positive function, for instance in virtue of their meaning-endowing potential, for deliberative democracy as part of the plurality of opinions within society. Religious and secular utterances cannot be clearly separated in any case, which for Habermas is a further pointer to the need for a process of mutual translation.

Habermas brought together his most important writings on the topic of religion between 2000 and 2005 in the volume *Zwischen Naturalismus und Religion* (2005; English translation: *Between Naturalism and Religion*, 2008). Particularly important in this connection is his essay on Immanuel Kant's understanding of religion. It is a lightly

7

revised version of his lecture "Wirkungsgeschichte und aktuellen Bedeutung von Kants Religionsphilosophie" ("On the Reception and Contemporary Importance of Kant's Philosophy of Religion"), which Habermas delivered at the Kant symposium at the Wiener Akademie der Wissenschaften in 2004, and in which he situates his own reflections within the tradition of the philosophy of religion. Here Habermas uncovers parallels and contrasts between the ways in which the relation between faith and knowledge is defined in Kant, Kierkegaard, Schleiermacher, and Hegel. The central point for him is that Kant, as he sees it, construes reason too broadly when he integrates the postulates of religious faith into its practical dimension. The justification of morality and that of the existence of God are fundamentally separate issues for Habermas. Thus he makes a clear distinction between faith and knowledge, as already in the Peace Prize speech and in the conversation with Cardinal Ratzinger. Hence philosophy must understand religion in the end as something external to it.

The lecture on Kant's philosophy of religion and on the location of his own reflection on religion within the history of philosophy formed the starting point for a further symposium in Vienna in 2005, in which Habermas discussed his interpretation of Kant's philosophy of religion with philosophers and theologians. Rudolf Langthaler and Herta Nagl-Docekal have published this multifaceted discussion under the title *Glauben und Wissen: Ein Symposium mit Jürgen Habermas über Religion* (Langthaler and Nagl-Docekal 2007).

Context and Location of the Essays in the Present Volume

The Peace Price speech, the conversation with Cardinal Ratzinger, and Habermas's reflections on the Kantian concept of religion are important starting points for the lecture of Habermas published in this volume.[3] Among other things, this lecture also contains Habermas's response to the address delivered by Benedict XVI on September 12, 2006 at the University of Regensburg. This address by the Pope aroused great interest especially on account of the interpretation of the relation between religion and violence in Islam which it presented. In the present essay Habermas deals with another aspect, namely the relation between faith and reason implied by the Pope's remarks.

In the Regensburg address, the Pope based his central point on a reading of the first line of the Gospel of St. John: "In the beginning was the Word." "Logos" means "reason" and "word." The basis of the world is accordingly a "reason" which is "capable of self-communication, precisely as reason," that is, in such a way that it can and should be rationally understood by its addressees.[4] Given this divine origin, reason acquires a "breadth" for theologians that enables it to adopt a critical stance towards tendencies to narrow its scope, as in modern scientism, for example. This critique does not need any guidance in principle from outside. It springs from the reason which unites human beings and which is capable of reflecting upon itself. Granted, the theologian understands this communicative dimension of the essence of reason ultimately as a self-communication (revelation) of its divine origin.

---

[3] A preliminary version of Habermas's contribution to the discussion was published on February 10, 2007 in the *Neue Zürcher Zeitung* under the title "Ein Bewusstsein von dem, was fehlt. Über Glauben und Wissen und den Defaitismus der modernen Vernunft" ("An Awareness of What is Missing: On Faith and Knowledge and Defeatism concerning Modern Reason").

[4] His understanding of Hellenization must also be interpreted in this sense. "Christian faith" and "Hellenic reason" formed a synthesis from the beginning. Thus Hellenization for Benedict XVI did not represent a belated development in the history of philosophy and theology, but an "an inner-biblical process which reaches its conclusion in the prologue to the Gospel of St. John. Thus the encounter between Athens and Jerusalem takes place already within the Bible." (On this see Ricken's contribution in the present volume.)

Nevertheless, he may introduce this understanding of reason in terms of revelation into the learned discourse, as tends to occur (or should occur), for example, at the university, where the different disciplines "[work] in everything on the basis of a single rationality with its various aspects." Here theology will be able to play its part in ensuring that "reason and faith come together in a new way."

Habermas also views this coming together as possible and he regards it as an urgent task. For, given the global challenges confronting humanity, the most important thing is to foster the willingness to communicate among human beings on the basis of a reason that unites them and possesses authority for them. However, nothing is more ominous than the refusal to communicate which we encounter on all sides today in the different forms of religious and ideological fundamentalism. Habermas's philosophy, his thought, and his personal engagement are devoted to working out the conditions of such a process of communication. In his recent writings, as in the present essay, Habermas consistently pays tribute to religious convictions and their profound historical traditions as powerful cognitive and motivational "potentials" which we cannot dispense with if this process of communication is to be successful.

However, for this two presuppositions must be fulfilled: "the religious side must accept the authority of 'natural' reason as the fallible results of the institutionalized sciences and the basic principles of universalistic egalitarianism in law and morality. Conversely, secular reason may not set itself up as the judge concerning truths of faith, even though in the end it can accept as reasonable only what it can translate into its own, in principle universally accessible, discourses." The goal cannot be simply to allow religious faith to be assimilated by "natural" reason. Habermas and the Pope are in complete agreement on this point. Yet what for the theologian is the self-communicating origin of our reason, and what makes it in principle receptive, must remain, along with what the theologian infers from it, strangely alien, indeed ultimately even unintelligible for the enlightened, "postmetaphysical" reason to which Habermas is wedded. However, the appearance that this signals the end of the conversation between faith and reason after all is misleading. For the insistence on this strangeness, indeed opacity of the religious contents from the perspective of enlightened reason must spur the theologian to offer a "reasonable" explication of what he means when he says that faith must not be assimilated by reason.[5]

Norbert Brieskorn's essay offers a commentary on Habermas's text entitled "On the Attempt to Recall a Relationship." He shows first that the lack in question should be understood as a *privatio*: "Reason lacks something which it could have but does not and which it painfully misses." He goes on to point out some facets of Habermas's concept of reason, thus of *that which is missing something* (i.e. reason). The third question which Brieskorn answers concerns *what is missing*. To judge from Habermas's remarks, this seems to be primarily religious rites, solidarity, and knowledge of "whether the political community is aware of being founded on secure and

---

[5] The formulation "awareness of what is missing," which Habermas chose for his title, brings to mind certain authors who exerted a major influence on his philosophy (our thanks to Norbert Brieskorn for numerous references). One could think, for example, of Ernst Bloch or Theodor W. Adorno, both of whom explored the "awareness of what is missing" in different ways. One can find several allusions to this in a radio conversation which they conducted in 1964 entitled "Something's Missing . . . On the Contradictions of Utopian Longing" (Bloch 1964). Here there is also an allusion to another thinker who could have been the inspiration for this formulation, namely Bertolt Brecht (in particular his libretto for *The Rise and Fall of the City Mahagonny*). Thomas Assheuer expressed this on the occasion of Habermas's sixty-fifth birthday as follows: "It is impossible to read Habermas without hearing Brecht's inner voice saying: 'Something's missing'." Finally, this formulation also, of course, contains an echo of Habermas's debate with Johann Baptist Metz, in particular with the latter's work *Memoria passionis: Ein provozierendes Gedächtnis in pluraler Gesellschaft* (Metz 2006).

resolute convictions concerning its legitimacy." At the same time, secular reason formulates clear demands on religion, above all concerning recognition of the authority of natural reason, of the egalitarianism of morality and law, and of the renunciation of violence. Brieskorn asks whether, in being confronted with these demands, religion is ultimately taken seriously or is dismissed as "backwards," which would not cohere with its self-understanding. Do Habermas's reflections amount to a *Tractatus theologico-politicus* for the twenty-first century, as Brieskorn asks in conclusion, alluding to Spinoza? This is certainly true in part, even if Habermas is less concerned about the institutional relation between Church and state than about the relation between reason and religion, and thus ultimately with an offer of discourse addressed by reason to the religious communities.

"How far can faith and reason be distinguished?" asks Michael Reder in his reflection on Habermas's remarks. As a first step he makes a plea for a broad understanding of religion. Religions, Reder argues, have always been parts of cultural processes and have assumed the most diverse reforms. A modern conception of religion must be attuned to religious diversity while at the same time also being able to thematize its ambivalence. Here it is also necessary to resist a functionalization of religion, for example by reducing it to a resource for endowing meaning. In a second step Reder shows to what extent Habermas's understanding of religion is geared to his distinction between norms and values, and goes on to make a plea for a much less sharp separation between these two domains. Reder addresses the implications of this for the relation between faith and reason in a third step. Drawing on the theory of knowledge and philosophy of religion of Nicholas of Cusa and that of Friedrich Schleiermacher, he argues for a stronger interconnection between faith and reason, through which the cultural expressions of religious forms can also ultimately be thematized. An associated recognition of the multivocal and rational character of religious expressions might also facilitate a constructive interreligious and inter-cultural discourse, especially when viewed from a global perspective.

Friedo Ricken takes as his starting point Habermas's proposed "translation" of the contents of religious belief into the language of enlightened reason. If the proposed translation is not to remain superficial and abstract, Ricken argues, then we must attend to what Habermas calls the "genealogy" of faith and reason that points to their common origin. This is the "lifeworld" in which both intellectual formations are rooted. Kant is presented as an example of how reason in its ultimate goals is connected with an act of trust [*Vertrauensvollzug*] which precedes it. Ricken offers a detailed treatment of Habermas's position on the Pope's critique of a modern reason which distances itself from faith. To this the Pope counterposes, according to Habermas, the ideal of a synthesis of Greek metaphysics and faith which is no longer viable in this form. According to Ricken, however, the Pope's primary concern is to draw attention to the fact that the connection with Greek phi-losophy can already be found in the earliest documents of Christianity, from which it follows that reason plays an indispensable role in the representation of the contents of faith. On the other hand, Ricken agrees with Habermas in his defense of Kant against the charge of narrowing reason in a scientistic way; for Kant is concerned precisely with a rational grounding of faith, even though not in the language of classical metaphysics. However, the latter is not simply invalid. It retains its importance as the form in which the early dogmas of the Christian faith were expressed, "[f]or anyone who wishes to replace the Greek concepts, as formulated, for example, by Nicaea and Chal-cedon, with different ones must prove that these other concepts capture the awkwardness and provocativeness of the biblical message as well as do the concepts of Greek metaphysics."

Josef Schmidt takes as his starting point the condition for the success of a dialogue between faith and reason highlighted by Habermas, namely that people must speak "with" and not "about" each other. The partners in dialogue should take each other seriously, in particular regarding their core convictions. They must assume at least the intelligibility of the latter and thus introduce their own convictions into the conversation in a "reasonable" manner. What the latter means for the person of faith is shown by three of her central convictions: God's uniqueness, human beings' likeness to God, and the certainty of ultimate security in God. When introduced into the conversation in a reasonable way, these contents prove to be "intelligible potentials" which remain a genuine challenge for an enlightened, non-scientistic mode of thought for which, as Habermas's philosophy demonstrates, reason is the unavoidable norm of genuine communication. Among these potentials are the justification of freedom through the orientation to the infinite God, his appearance in this openness to him, and the certainty of ultimate security in this connection with him. However, the intelligibility of these contents also implies that they cannot be cognitively grasped through theory; thus they can be assimilated only through an act of trust which is, in turn, an enduring moment of the exercise of freedom.

The volume concludes with Habermas's reply to these contributions. This is a further reflection of the fact that the volume is the record of a discussion, of the exploration of shared perspectives, and of the uncovering of approaches to the interpretation of religion and of its social importance.

The question of how societies will develop during the twenty-first century and of the challenges that this will pose in the light of global dynamics must remain largely open. However, it is more than probable that religion will play a decisive role in these (global) social processes. Viewed against this background, the following essays are intended as contributions to this open discussion.

2
An Awareness of What is Missing

JÜRGEN HABERMAS

On April 9, 1991, a memorial service for Max Frisch was held in St Peter's Church in Zürich. It began with Karin Pilliod, Frisch's partner, reading out a brief declaration written by the deceased. It stated, among other things: "We let our nearest speak, and without an 'amen.' I am grateful to the ministers of St. Peter's in Zürich . . . for their permission to place the coffin in the church during our memorial service. The ashes will be strewn some-where." Two friends spoke. No priest, no blessing. The mourners were made up of intellectuals, most of whom had little time for church and religion. Frisch himself had drawn up the menu for the meal that followed. At the time the ceremony did not strike me as peculiar. However, its form, place, and progression *were* peculiar. Clearly, Max Frisch, an agnostic who rejected any profession of faith, had sensed the awkwardness of non-religious burial practices and, by his choice of place, publicly declared that the enlightened modern age has failed to find a suitable replacement for a religious way of coping with the final *rite de passage* which brings life to a close.

One can interpret this gesture as an expression of mel-ancholy over something which has been irretrievably lost. Yet one can also view the ceremony as a paradoxical event which tells us something about secular reason, namely that it is unsettled by the opaqueness of its merely apparently

15

clarified relation to religion. At the same time, the church, even Zwingli's reformed church, also had to overcome its inhibitions when it allowed this ceremony, given its secular character "without an 'amen'," to take place within its hallowed halls. The philosophically enlightened self-understanding of modernity stands in a peculiar dialectical relationship to the theological self-understanding of the major world religions, which intrude into this modernity as the most awkward element from its past.

It is not a question of an unstable compromise between irreconcilable elements. We should not try to dodge the alternative between an anthropocentric orientation and the view from afar of theocentric or cosmocentric thinking. However, it makes a difference whether we speak with one another or merely about one another. If we want to avoid the latter, two presuppositions must be fulfilled: the religious side must accept the authority of "natural" reason as the fallible results of the institutionalized sciences and the basic principles of universalistic egalitarianism in law and morality. Conversely, secular reason may not set itself up as the judge concerning truths of faith, even though in the end it can accept as reasonable only what it can translate into its own, in principle universally accessible, discourses. The one presupposition is no more trivial from a theological perspective than the other is from that of philosophy.

Modern science compelled a philosophical reason which had become self-critical to break with metaphysical constructions of the totality of nature and history. With this advance in reflection, nature and history became the preserve of the empirical sciences and not much more was left for philosophy than the general competences of knowing, speaking, and acting subjects. With this the synthesis of faith and knowledge forged in the tradition extending from Augustine to Thomas fell apart. Although modern philosophy assimilated the Greek heritage critically in the form of an, if you will, "postmetaphysical" thinking, at the same time it discarded Judeo-Christian

16

sacred knowledge [*Heilswissen*]. While it acknowledges metaphysics as belonging to the prehistory of its own emergence, it treats revelation and religion as something alien and extraneous. In spite of this rejection, however, religion remains present in a different way to the metaphysics which has been outgrown. The cleavage between secular knowledge and revealed knowledge cannot be bridged. Yet the perspective from which postmetaphysical thinking approaches religion shifts once secular reason takes seriously the shared origin of philosophy and religion in the revolution in worldviews of the Axial Age (around the middle of the first millennium BCE).

Although metaphysical thinking worked out a division of labor with Christianity over the course of western history which enabled it to withdraw from the administration of the means of salvation pursued through contemplation, in its Platonic beginnings philosophy also offered its followers a similar contemplative promise of salvation to that of the other cosmocentric "intellectual religions" of the East (Max Weber). Viewed from the perspective of the cognitive advance from *mythos* to *logos*, metaphysics can be situated on the same level as all of the worldviews which emerged at that time, including Mosaic monotheism. Each of them made it possible to take a synoptic view of the world as a whole from a transcendent point of view and to distinguish the flood of phenomena from the underlying essences. Moreover, reflection on the place of the individual in the world gave rise to a new awareness of historical contingency and of the responsibility of the acting subject. However, if religious and metaphysical worldviews prompted similar learning processes, then both modes, faith and knowledge, together with their traditions based respectively in Jerusalem and Athens, belong to the history of the origins of the secular reason which today provides the medium in which the sons and daughters of modernity communicate concerning their place in the world.

This modern reason will learn to understand itself only when it clarifies its relation to a contemporary religious consciousness which has become reflexive by grasping the shared origin of the two complementary intellectual formations in the cognitive advance of the Axial Age. In speaking of complementary intellectual formations, I am expressly rejecting two positions: first, the blinkered enlightenment which is unenlightened about itself and which denies religion any rational content, but also, second, Hegel's view for which religion represents an intellectual formation worthy of being recalled, but only in the form of a "representational thinking" [*vorstellendes Denken*] which is subordinate to philosophy. Faith remains opaque for knowledge in a way which may neither be denied nor simply accepted. This reflects the inconclusive nature of the confrontation between a self-critical reason which is willing to learn and contemporary religious convictions. This confrontation can sharpen post-secular society's awareness of the unexhausted force [*das Unabgegoltene*] of religious traditions. Secularization functions less as a filter separating out the contents of traditions than as a transformer which redirects the flow of tradition.

My motive for addressing the issue of faith and knowledge is to mobilize modern reason against the defeatism lurking within it. Postmetaphysical thinking cannot cope on its own with the defeatism concerning reason which we encounter today both in the postmodern radicalization of the "dialectic of the Enlightenment" and in the naturalism founded on a naive faith in science. It is different with a practical reason that despairs of the motivating power of its good reasons without the backing of the history of philosophy, because a modernization threatening to spin out of control tends to counteract rather than to complement the precepts of its morality of justice.

Practical reason provides justifications for the universalistic and egalitarian concepts of morality and law which shape the freedom of the individual and interpersonal relations in a normatively plausible way. However, the decision to engage in action based on solidarity when faced with threats which can be averted only by collective efforts calls for more than insight into good reasons. Kant wanted to make good this weakness of rational morality through the assurances of his philosophy of religion. However, this same strict rational morality explains why enlightened reason unavoidably loses its grip on the images, preserved by religion, of the moral whole – of the Kingdom of God on earth – as collectively binding ideals. At the same time, practical reason fails to fulfill its own vocation when it no longer has sufficient strength to awaken, and to keep awake, in the minds of secular subjects, an awareness of the violations of solidarity throughout the world, an awareness of what is missing, of what cries out to heaven.

Could an altered perspective on the genealogy of reason rescue postmetaphysical thinking from this dilemma? At any rate, it throws a different light on that reciprocal learning process in which the political reason of the liberal state and religion are already involved. This touches on conflicts which are currently being triggered around the world by the unexpected spiritual renewal and by the unsettling political role of religious communities. Apart from Hindu nationalism, Islam and Christianity are the main sources of this disturbance.

From the standpoint of their geographical expansion, the winners are not the nationally organized religious communities, such as the Protestant Churches in Germany and Britain, but the Catholic world Church and, above all, the Evangelicals and the Muslims with their decentralized networks and globally operating movements. The former are spreading in Latin America, China, South Korea, and in the Philippines, whereas the latter are extending from the Middle East both into sub-Saharan Africa and into Southeast Asia, where Indonesia has the largest Muslim population. This resurgence is going hand-in-hand with an increase in the frequency of conflicts between different religious groups and denominations. Even though many of these conflicts have different origins, they become inflamed when they are codified in religious terms. Since September 11, 2001, the main issue has been the political instrumentalization of Islam. However, without the *Kulturkampf* of the religious right, even George W. Bush would not have won a majority for the policy which Thomas Assheuer has described as an aggressive alliance of democracy export and neoliberalism.

The mentality of the hard core of the "born-again Christians" is marked by a fundamentalism founded on a literal interpretation of holy scripture. This mindset, whether we encounter it in Islamic, Christian, Jewish, or Hindu form, clashes with fundamental convictions of modernity. The conflicts are sparked at the political level by the neutrality of the state towards worldviews, that is, by equal freedom of religion for all and by the emancipation of science from religious authority. Similar conflicts dominated large parts of modern European history; today they are being repeated not only in relations between the western and Islamic worlds but also in those between militant groups of religious and secularized citizens within liberal societies. We can view these conflicts either as power struggles between state authority and religious movements or as conflicts between secular and religious convictions.

Viewed in terms of power politics, the state which is neutral towards worldviews can be content with the mere conformity of the religious communities to a legally imposed freedom of religion and science. The position of the Catholic Church in Europe until the Second Vatican Council, for example, was marked by conformity. However, the liberal state cannot be content with such a *modus vivendi*, and not simply on account of the instability of such an enforced arrangement. For, as a constitutional democracy, it depends on a mode of legitimation founded on convictions.

In order to acquire this legitimation, it requires the support of reasons which can be accepted in a pluralist society by religious citizens, by citizens of different religions, and by secular citizens alike. The constitutional state must not only act neutrally towards worldviews but it must also rest on normative foundations which can be justified neutrally towards worldviews – and that means in postmetaphysical terms. The religious communities cannot turn a deaf ear to this normative requirement. This is why those complementary learning process in which the secular and the religious sides involve one another come into play here.

Instead of grudging accommodation to externally imposed constraints, the content of religion must open itself up to the normatively grounded expectation that it should recognize for reasons of its own the neutrality of the state towards worldviews, the equal freedom of all religious communities, and the independence of the institutionalized sciences. This is a momentous step. For it is not just a matter of renouncing political force and religious indoctrination as means of imposing religious truths; it is also a matter of religious consciousness becoming reflexive when confronted with the necessity of relating its articles of faith to competing systems of belief and to the scientific monopoly on the production of factual knowledge.

Conversely, however, the secular state, which, with its contractual legal legitimation, functions as an intellectual formation and not merely as an empirical power, must also face the question of whether it is imposing asymmetrical obligations on its religious citizens. For the liberal state guarantees the equal freedom to exercise religion not only as a means of upholding law and order but also for the normative reason of protecting the freedom of belief and conscience of everyone. Thus it may not demand anything of its religious citizens which cannot be reconciled with a life that is led authentically "from faith."

May the state require these citizens to split their existence into public and private parts, for example by obliging them to justify their stances in the political arena exclusively in terms of non-religious reasons? Or should the obligation to employ a worldview-neutral language hold instead only for politicians who make legally binding decisions within the institutions of state? If religiously justified stances are accorded a legitimate place in the public sphere, however, the political community officially recognizes that religious utterances can make a meaningful contribution to clarifying controversial questions of principle.

This not only raises the question of the subsequent translation of their rational content into a publicly accessible language. Rather, the liberal state must also expect its secular citizens, in exercising their role as citizens, not to treat religious expressions as simply irrational. Given the spread of a naturalism based on a naive faith in science, this presupposition cannot be taken for granted. The rejection of secularism is anything but a trivial matter. It touches in turn on our initial question of how modern reason, which has turned its back on metaphysics, should understand its relation to religion. Of course, the expectation that theology should engage seriously with postmetaphysical thinking is by no means trivial either.

In his recent address in Regensburg, Pope Benedict XVI interpreted the old controversy over the Hellenization and de-Hellenization of Christianity in a way which is unexpectedly critical of modernity. In doing so he also answered the question of whether Christian theology must wrestle with the challenges of modern, postmetaphysical reason in the negative. The Pope appeals to the synthesis of Greek metaphysics and biblical faith forged in the tradition extending from Augustine to Thomas, and he implicitly denies that there are good reasons for the polarization between faith and knowledge which became an empirical feature of European modernity. Although he criticizes the view that one must "[put] the clock back to the time before the Enlightenment and [reject] the insights of the modern age," he resists the power of the arguments which shattered that worldview synthesis.

However, the move from Duns Scotus to nominalism does not merely lead to the Protestant voluntarist deity [*Willensgott*] but also paves the way for modern natural science. Kant's transcendental turn leads not only to a critique of the proofs of God's existence but also to the concept of autonomy which first made possible our modern European understanding of law and democracy. Moreover, historicism does not necessarily lead to a relativistic self-denial of reason. As a child of the Enlightenment, it makes us sensitive to cultural differences and prevents us from over-generalizing context-dependent judgments. *Fides quaerens intellectum* ("faith seeking understanding") – regardless of how welcome the search for the rational core of faith may be, it seems to me that it is not helpful to ignore those three stages in the process of de-Hellenization which have contributed to the modern self-understanding of secular reason when tracing the genealogy of the "shared reason" of people of faith, unbelievers, and members of different religions.

3
On the Attempt to Recall a Relationship

NORBERT BRIESKORN, S. J.

On an initial reading, Jürgen Habermas's essay "An Aware-ness of What is Missing" shows us that reason has a social concern and, at the same time, that it recognizes that it cannot accomplish this social task alone. Hence it must look for helpers, for willing allies, and it thinks it can find them among the religious communities. These communi-ties are marked by their vitality and vigor, which is the reason for enlisting their aid; they are issued invitations and requirements are made of them; the rules of the game must be explained to them. The aspiration to such an alli-ance of convenience revives memories. Political communi-ties have seized upon religion more than once: Rome invoked its own and foreign gods before and after the defeat of Cannae, Constantine invoked the Christian God at the Milvian Bridge, and Stalin invoked the Orthodox Church when planning the "Great Patriotic War." Alli-ances of convenience in general, and these ones in particu-lar, have an air of mutual betrayal. They can be marked by belated remorse, when the same power which forges the alliance previously persecuted the religious communi-ties or declared their death or their supersession. There is no lack of theories for justifying such alliances either: in the *Discorsi*, Machiavelli declared that religions, with the exception of the Christian religion, are necessary in order to reinforce the spirit of resistance and the willingness to fight; and at the end of the fourth book of *Du contrat social*, Jean-Jacques Rousseau purports to offer a conclusive demonstration that the expectation of a Last Judgment alone can discipline the people.

On a closer examination, Habermas's article impresses that it is not the state which issues the call to form alliances but reason, and that religious communities are supposed to come to the aid of reason, not to that of the state. As the title "An Awareness of What is Missing" suggests, Habermas is speaking from the standpoint of reason and in the name of reason. Reason is pursuing its own aims.

Before examining what this involves, we must first address three questions: What is meant in general by saying "that something is missing": Who exactly is missing what? And: What is missing? Only then can we inquire how this lack may be overcome, offset, or endured.

What Kind of Lack Are We Talking About?

When people say that something is "missing," they can mean one of two things: a person may lack wings, or she may lack eyesight. In the first case the person is not impaired in her humanity. Indeed, we even have to say that if she had what is missing she would no longer be human. In this case we speak of "negation": a human being is not an *animal volabile*, a bird, after all. However, she can lack eyesight and that impairs her bodily life as a human being, even though she certainly does not thereby lose her human dignity and nature. Traditionally one spoke in the latter case not of *negatio*, but of *privatio*. Only in the second case is genuine regret appropriate, and only in this case are aid, correction, and replacement possibilities, even if the essence of the human being is not diminished. To repeat, it is completely out of place for a human being to regret not being an angel, but one may very well wish to regain one's sight (see Suárez 2002, pp. 380f., 536 ff., and 570 ff.). Habermas is concerned with the

25

second case, that is, deficiency in the sense of *privatio*. Reason lacks something which it could have but does not and which it painfully misses. It lacks something which belongs to it and is part of its constitution.

We must differentiate within this second alternative in turn. Two cases can arise. On the one hand, it could be that reason had something at one time, but lost it: it is aware of a loss. Consciousness has not become poorer, but nevertheless it regrets a loss. On the other hand, it could be like examining a room which has not yet been filled with the foreseen objects and noticing the empty places which remain to be filled. The question is whether reason has lost something and wants to recover it, indeed must recover it, or whether it is developing towards a completion which it has never known and into which it wants to mature. Habermas's text reveals that in this case it is a question of the first rather than the second alternative. Its losses will appear different depending on how we construe the concept of reason. Only minor losses occur if the concept of reason is very "parsimonious"; the losses are grave, by contrast, if a very elevated and strong conception of reason is assumed. But have we not perhaps over-estimated reason? If yes, one would speak of the first alternative sketched above, namely that it lacks something to which it is not at all entitled. I only want to pose this question without pursuing it further here.

Who is Missing Something?

Habermas speaks of modern reason. What is meant in the following sentences by this perhaps so trite and common-place, and hence murky, concept?

Reason – by which is meant practical reason – is the faculty that wants to orient human life to a final horizon, and this more in a general and fundamental way than in detail, where reason also takes the conditions of the orientation into consideration. Thus reason would not be merely the power which determines a social form of life in an ethical and legal sense but also shows it to be guided by principles, but which – now breaking with Kant's program (see *Critique of Pure Reason*, B 823, p. 672) – not only seeks to guard against errors concerning the conduct of life but also to discover the truth concerning life and to feed it into social life. To these conditions also belongs the fact that reason, on the human side, involves participating in the one reason and that those who participate are fallible, finite beings who are in many respects needy and in many ways open to improvement. This participating reason should know this and take it into consideration. It must take the "veto" of reality seriously if it is not to fall into error and to commit itself to too little or too much. This participating reason can overtax or undertax human beings; it can assume that they are endowed with a form of self-possession which they never had or with an incapacity which they falsely assume to be insurmountable. In orienting itself to as much reason, it has the power to correct.

To return once again to reason as such: Kant drew attention to its search for unity (*Critique of Pure Reason*, B 714, p. 614), which demands that "every connection in the world," including each of my opinions and thoughts, should be ordered "as if it had sprouted from the intention of a highest reason." This reason is, exists, and develops in different dimensions: first that of transcendence, second that of the orientation to the world, third that of history, and finally that of discursive rationality (which means that we include the understanding). Reason can encounter faith in each of the four dimensions – it can, though it need not. The encounter assumes a different form depending on the dimension in question. In the first case, it assumes the form of the striving towards the unconditional which, on the religious side, can ultimately manifest itself as a God who can be addressed in the second person. In the second case it assumes the form of acts of solidarity with our planet and with human society, where religions can either reinforce the asymmetrical relations or foster those of selfless aid. It takes the form, third, of respect for the past and of preparation for the future, of emphasizing that nobody and nothing will be forgotten and that each person must take responsibility for him or herself; and finally, fourth, of the doctrinal treatment of articles of faith.

Precisely when we understand "reason" as open to development in this sense, then instead of "reason" we should say (focusing only on the outside of the inside, as it were, and again closer to Habermas's approach): "the freely reached consensus of free citizens" (Anacker 1974, p. 1603). Here I would like to add that, no matter how helpful and indispensable it is to reconstruct and to test validity intersubjectively and also to affirm the result in an intersubjectively justified way (for what use is a theoretical affirmation when it does not lead to communal practice?), and no matter how much the consensus fosters social peace and provides evidence, nevertheless it is overtaxed by the business of truth, for that is not its business. Anyone who appeals to such agreements as an ultimate foundation brings a (his) human product into play – specifically, consensus – which is itself in need of justification and for this very reason is also capable of being justified in a meaningful world; the path to such a justification, and the justification itself, are in need of confirmation (Habermas 1991b, p. 38). Do the discursive procedure and consensus reveal something, spelt out in large letters as it were, which is not made clear by the small type of the participating reason? Does it perhaps become clearer that the discourse community with and in spite of its intersubjective mediation and its knowledge of unconditional factors[1] has not outstripped "a subjectivity understood in radically individualistic terms" (Ebeling 1990, p. 20), or is this

---

[1] By which is meant the unconditionality of propositions whose truth is asserted, furthermore the unconditional duty of intelligibility, the unconditional goodness of the imperative, and the duty of unconditional truthfulness (see Habermas 2001).

assumption mistaken? Does participating reason take our mortality[2] and the *nexus animarum* into consideration – the interconnectedness of all human beings with and among one another which can neither be denied nor studied in all of its relations – a *nexus* in which aid is received from both acquaintances and strangers and strength drawn from those both close and distant?

Let me make a further observation concerning Habermas's concept of reason. Reason sees itself as a social process and, as the article makes clear, in a social dimension. In Spinoza's *Tractatus theologico-politicus*, reason is conceived without a social and historical dimension, but these dimensions are characteristic features of religion (Spinoza 2007, ch. 14).

What is missing?

The answer to this question can be found in passages from Habermas's article:

1. A rite is missing which copes with "the final *rite de passage* which brings life to a close." To express this as a reproach: This modern reason does not take the finitude, the mortality, or – to put it even more precisely and from the perspective of belief in immortality – this transformation of human life sufficiently seriously, or at any rate it leaves this "phase" to itself, or even suppresses it altogether. Can modern reason incorporate this "element"?

2. There is a lack of solidarity and of motivation to show solidarity. Habermas writes: "At the same time, practical reason fails to fulfill its own vocation when it no longer has sufficient strength to awaken, and to keep awake, in the minds of secular subjects, an awareness of the violations of solidarity throughout the world,

[2] Reason must be understood from the perspective of the human as a mortal being (see Ebeling 1990, p. 28).

an awareness of what is missing, of what cries out to heaven." Thus modern reason would have to over-come its individualistic character by transforming itself into a reason which understands itself in inter-subjective terms and is aware of its responsibility (towards whom?).

3. There is a lack of reliable knowledge concerning whether the political community is aware of being founded on secure and robust convictions concerning its legitimacy. Habermas attaches great value to such a contribution, perhaps as much as to the contribution to solidarity which must be realized at the global level. Religious communities must contribute to legit-imizing, supporting, and strengthening their own, national political communities. To the preoccupation with reviving a dormant solidarity, not least in favour of benefit of the Developing World, is added the further concern with strengthening one's own politi-cal community. Attention shifts from the world society to the state, the nation-state. This reflects a correct perception that certain religious communities feel greater responsibility for the "world" than for their own political community, that they prefer to focus their activity on distant places than to deal with tasks in their own national home. Machiavelli and Rousseau reproached Christians, not without a certain degree of justification, with such a lack of interest in the political community and with taking refuge in distant concerns.[3]

---

[3] A reference to Joseph Ratzinger's position on the state during the 1980s is appropriate here. Ratzinger acknowledged responsibility for the state and highlighted its factual or always possible demonic power [*Dämonie*], its susceptibility to seduction and unlimited mani-pulability. This stance of Ratzinger's was influenced by Augustine's *City of God*. At the time Ratzinger did not insist that such a form of state must be reformed into a republican, constitutional state, but that the institution of the (holy) Church alone is capable of resisting such demonic power (see Ratzinger 1982, 2008).

4. There is also a lack of "religiously justified stances . . . in the public sphere." It would do reason no harm to recognize the history of the process through which it achieved consciousness, not in order to live in future in accordance with models of the past, but in order to define its position here and now.

Defeatism or Practical Resignation?

Thus here we can pose the question of whether this defeat-ism[4] is a momentary feeling that may come over one under the impression of certain facts, or in the light of certain historical developments, but which can pass away again; or whether we are dealing here with a weakness which remains as a weakness, perhaps becoming even more pronounced, an exposed flank which belongs to its basic constitution and which, although one would like to see it strengthened, must in the end be tolerated and accepted.

Those who analyze history with Auguste Comte's three-stage schema in mind[5] will be aware of the three historical stages which must be passed through, the route which must be followed, and was followed during the twentieth century, which leads from the theological, via the metaphysical, to the positive, sociological era – a schema which allows neither for reversal nor for repetition.

[4] Defeatism is paraphrased as "the inclination and endeavor to bring a war to an end as soon as possible, also under unfavorable circumstances, which springs from a lack of confidence in the possibility of victory, or which takes hold as a result of the length of the war and of military setbacks . . . According to communist ideology, someone is a defeatist who doubts the effectiveness of party and government policy or of economic policy" (*Der große Brockhaus* 1953, p. 79).

[5] The theological era, according to Comte, is superseded by the metaphysical era, and this in turn by the positive era, that is, the era of sociology (Comte 1997, pp. 71–2). Each phase was necessary, the second could not be skipped, and he regarded the third as definitive. For Comte, neither can there be a return to the two previous phases nor can they recur in a different guise.

As a matter of fact, the passage of time and the changes it brings never allow a past state to be recovered. Thus, as regards Habermas's concept of reason, we would be dealing, as a result of the historical development, with a definitive and irrevocably positive reason (an *a*-theological and *a*-metaphysical reason) – thus with a concept of reason which, as we have seen, Habermas does not make his own.

Admittedly Comte's scheme represents a human view of human history, and hence is fallible and subject to error; nevertheless one can discover genuine, enduring obligations within it, namely not to fall back into tutelage, to be self-determining, and not to allow oneself to be bossed around. For the remainder, in Habermas's reflections we encounter a peculiarly intricate relationship between recollection and suppression. On the one hand, it helps reason to recognize its one-time proximity to religion and metaphysics. Thus reason does not blindly invite the religious communities to become involved in the space of society, but does so in an awareness of the prehistory. Towards these communities, in turn, the past does not become a reason for ostracism and exclusion.

In the present essay, as already in the speech in the Paulskirche, reason addresses demands to the religious communities (there is no mention of demands in the opposite direction). All religious communities must acknowledge certain demands. Habermas names three: "The religious side must accept the authority of 'natural' reason as the fallible results of the institutionalized sciences and the basic principles of universalistic egalitarianism in law and morality." The renunciation of violence in social relations and between communities founded on worldviews must be required of religious communities.

The requirements which "a reason anxious about its relation to religion" thus addresses to the religious communities do not affect the domain of articles of faith and of the practice of faith. Scientific results can never take on the quality of religious dogmas, as the reference to fallibility already implies. Law should never become the sole instrument of social regulation any more than morality should; and it needs to be supplemented by mercy, love. State law should never force someone to perform an action which clashes with his conscience.

A postscript: The three demands outlined are not addressed specifically to religious communities *qua* religious communities, but are addressed to all human beings. However, just because they are intended as conditions of entry into the public arena, these demands brand their addressees as retrograde, as not up to date and as "backward."

And the Religious Communities Themselves?

Against the hopeful view on the vitality of religious communities of a reason which takes itself to be realistic it must be objected that the egoistic way of life also within religious communities has hollowed out the way of life in solidarity with others and has rendered it powerless. Even though Herbert Marcuse once tried to identify "islands" and "enclaves" of the successful life within the alienated, exploited society (Marcuse 1971), one will not in general find that religious communities are free of egoism and of deficient solidarity.

The sons and daughters of modernity do not live outside of the religious communities. To assume this would be to fall back behind a level of differentiation which already enabled Aurelius Augustinus to identify and to acknowledge the porosity and intermingling of the *civitates*. The fact that members of such communities bring a critical collective awareness to bear on egoisms does not rectify the evil.

Those who examine their social surroundings will see that there is an "accommodating" movement, indeed one which has long been operative, with varying intensity and spurts throughout the twentieth century. It is a search, even a struggle, for the answer to the question of the correct relation between politics and religion (see Thierse 2000, in particular the articles by Haunhorst and Werbick).

Here I cannot present a seamless history of this search. Controversial starting positions are expressed in the slogan "Religion is a private matter!" and by the narrow institutional intermeshing and guarantee of a throne–altar relation. The Christian religion – to which I can confine myself here – inherently demands that we should become active through works, and hence must not ignore that work which has the most profound effects on human lives, namely politics. Even though we cannot derive detailed blueprints for politics from the message of revelation itself, it traces out certain guidelines which are useful and, from the perspective of faith (though only from this perspective), also obligatory as cornerstones of politics. Among these are the concern for human beings, global responsibility, the discourse concerning a salvation which is not exhausted in social commitment and concerning a God who offers himself gratuitously without first demanding services from human beings, etc.

Thus a commitment is required from the side of the Churches, in and following the dissolution of the burdensome institutional linkage, which respects this distance, which goes beyond the preoccupation with one's own religious life for its own sake. A gospel for life (John 10.10: "I came that they may have life, and have it abundantly") will also speak for the political communal life.

A *Tractatus theologico-politicus* for the Twenty-First Century?

Juxtaposing the article to other statements by Jürgen Habermas on the relation between reason and religious communities reveals that they address and answer, in a certain sense at least, central points for the twenty-first century which were the subject of classical "theological-political tracts."

Characteristic of Habermas's "Tractatus" is that it does not contain an examination of forms of the state because constitutional democracy is assumed to be self-evident; unlike Spinoza in 1670 in his *Tractatus theologico-politicus*, Habermas does not distinguish between Churches and sects, and he does not assume, in contrast to many theological-political tracts from European history, that religion is necessary for the many, whereas reason is sufficient for the few, the intellectual elite. Nor is the state accorded any role as arbitrator over the contents of religious communities, much less are the latter placed under state control. There cannot be a state Church. Reason does not presume to act as judge concerning truths of faith and it does not require that religion should be truncated into socially useful morality. The impotence of reason is revealed by the fact that it never knows whether, and how sincerely, the members of religious communities take these requirements to heart. The protection of human rights and the freedom of the religious communities to organize themselves must be guaranteed no less than the limitations placed on religious communities by generally valid laws. This and much more is obvious for Habermas and for reasonable readers.

According to Spinoza, the political community needs religion; in Habermas, reason has need of the religious communities. His aim is not to develop a kind of blueprint for state–Church relations, but to extend an invitation to the religious communities. That it is expressed in this way and not otherwise reflects the recoguition of the power of a powerlessness.

4

How Far Can Faith and Reason Be Distinguished?

Remarks on Ethics and the Philosophy of Religion

MICHAEL REDER

Today religions play a perceptible and at times an important social role in many societies. In recent years a lively scholarly and social discussion has begun over how this development should be described and explained. The eleventh of September 2001 and the ensuing global developments have lent additional impetus to the discussion of religions. In addition, religions are increasingly being thematized by (political) philosophy as parts of global processes, as in the reflections of Jacques Derrida, Michael Walzer, and Richard Rorty.

Over the past decade, Jürgen Habermas has repeatedly offered answers to these questions and in the process has made an essential contribution to stimulating the discussion. Arguing from the perspective of the theory of deliberative democracy, he places particular emphasis on the importance of a redemptive appropriation of religious meaning potentials in a generally accessible language. Religions, as part of the public sphere, should be heeded when negotiating controversial normative questions, for they possess a significant potential for justifying normative questions and are an important source of motivation for citizens to participate in negotiation processes. To this end, Habermas requires that religious and secular citizens should demonstrate a complementary willingness to learn how to translate the arguments into their respective languages.

The following remarks are intended as a commentary on Habermas's reflections on the social importance of religion. Their aim is, first, to examine how Habermas situates religions within social theory and, taking this as a starting point, to explore perspectives in ethics and in the philosophy of religion. In each of the three directions, the intention is to offer proposals concerning how, starting from Habermas's reflections, the discussion concerning the (global) social role of religions can be taken further.

Plea for a Broad Understanding of Religion

With his concept of the "post-secular," Habermas has exercised a major influence on the discussion concerning the social significance of religions in recent years. The concept expresses the fact that modern societies not only have to gear themselves to the continued existence of religion, but that religions actively shape social life at different levels and in a variety of forms. Thus religions continue to play an important role even in liberal societies.

This definition of modern societies as postsecular correlates with a number of other aspects of Habermas's social analysis. Among other things, the attention he has devoted to globalization and to bioethics in recent years has led him to take a rather skeptical view of current social developments. As regards globalization, we can observe, on Habermas's analysis, an "unmastered dynamics" of the world economy and world society which until now could not be tamed by supranational political processes. At the same time, at the national level we are encountering a diminishing sensibility for social pathologies. Modernity, on Habermas's analysis, is in danger of "spinning out of control." The liberal state, in particular, which depends on the solidarity of its citizens and their motivation to participate in public discourses, finds itself confronted with this problem. Sources of motivation "could dry up as a result of an 'uncontrolled' secularization of society as a whole" (Habermas 2008, p. 102) – or that, at least, is the fear. This would jeopardize the project of deliberative democracy in its very foundations.

We must ask, first, whether, as the concept "*post*-secular" indirectly assumes, religions have indeed experienced such a loss in importance during the modern period. Today it is emphasized with increasing regularity that religions played an important social role in the process of secularization, albeit in other guises. Secularization is not and has never been a linear process, as Hans Joas, for instance, objects, which is why concepts such as "secular" and "post-secular" seem problematic (Joas 2008). Especially from a global perspective, the concept of secularization (interpreted in linear terms) is convincing only with qualification as a description of global social developments. Thus people often speak of an enhanced visibility of religions.

Habermas's analysis is convincing in that our era is marked by an increase in violent conflicts, by an enduring pronounced disparity between North and South, and by asymmetrical power structures. However, this is also counterbalanced by certain positive global developments. From an economic point of view, formerly poor developing countries have experienced an upswing and, notwithstanding its provisional character and justified criticism, a start has been made in constructing an institutional framework for the global economy. The multiplicity of regional and globally active nongovernmental organizations is also a pointer to a global public arena and a reflection of a political consciousness which aspires to a just reform of global structures. This is not intended to encourage a naively positive interpretation of global reality but to emphasize that globalization should be interpreted in principle as an ambivalent process (Reder 2006). Religions are themselves part of this ambivalence. In certain regions they have positive effects (for example, in promoting peace and combating poverty); in other areas they are more likely to foster conflict or reinforce asymmetrical power structures (see Müller 2007).

When global developments are viewed primarily from the perspective of their spinning out of control, the attention to religion is in danger of being instrumentalized. Religions are supposed to help to prevent or to overcome social disruptions where they occur. Habermas tends to instrumentalize religions for this kind of reflexive treatment of the moral problems of modernity (see Danz 2007). This tendency becomes apparent in his functional definition of religion. Religions for him have in the first place the social function of a moral resource, when modern societies are no longer able to tap into a motivational source for their normative principles. Habermas himself points out that his intention is not to reduce religion to a single function. His choice of the example of the funeral of Max Frisch also suggests as much, for there it was primarily a matter of coping with contingency through ritual and less of providing normative foundations for the modern constitutional state. Religions perform a range of social functions of which providing ethical worldviews is just one. Shaping cultural life, coping with contingency, and the thematization of the relation between transcendence and immanence are further functions of religions, and only a synoptic view provides a detailed picture of their social importance. Thus morality – here one can agree completely with Friedrich Schleiermacher's view in his *On Religion: Speeches to its Cultural Despisers* – is just one aspect to which religions should not be reduced. In addition, many religions would resist such a reduction, something which likewise constitutes an argument for a broad understanding of religion.

The multidimensionality of religions also deserves attention in another respect. For Habermas's line of argument implies an understanding of religion which is geared in the first instance to the "religions of the Axial Age." Given the pluralism of western societies, and in particular also given the diversity of religious–cultural hybrid forms, it is important from a global perspective, especially for liberal thought, not to be misled by a conceptual narrowing into neglecting the importance of these forms of religion.[1]

Habermas stands in the Kantian tradition and, in spite of all differentiations, he shares the connection which Kant makes between religion and morality, albeit in a markedly more guarded version. As a political philosopher who argues from the perspective of the theory of deliberation, he is mainly interested in the moral importance of religions in public negotiation processes. However, it seems to be especially important and prudent to broaden our understanding of religion if we want to do justice to the diversity of religions (and of quasi-religious hybrid forms) in social discourses and not to focus exclusively on certain moral expressions of religions.

Situating Religion Within the Domain of Ethical Worldviews

In order to be able to transform our understanding of religion in this way, we need to reflect on the definition of the relation between faith and reason, for Habermas's reflection on religion turns on this relation, both at the level of ethics and at that of the philosophy of religion. This was already apparent in his Peace Prize speech, though also in his debate with the former Cardinal Ratzinger and in the present contribution. As regards its content, his interpretation of the relation between faith

---

[1] This becomes especially clear in the controversy with Wittgenstein when Habermas remarks critically on the conclusions which can be drawn from a broad concept of religion (which draws on Wittgenstein): "The semantic closure of incommensurable language games grants esoteric doctrines equal status alongside religions and natural scientific theories" (Habermas 2007b, p. 385) – Habermas thinks that this, in particular, is not reasonable in the light of reflection on religion.

and reason is especially discernible from his reflections on Kant's concept of religion (Habermas 2008, pp. 209–47). At the heart of these reflections is the idea that Kant traces the boundaries of mere reason too broadly when he wants to justify the assumption of God's existence along with morality. Postmetaphysical thinking, by contrast, should understand religion as something external to it. Philosophy should not presume to know what is at stake in religion. Faith and reason instead represent two incommensurable intellectual forms which are clearly separate from one another. Hence philosophy can at most reconstruct the contents of religions in a universally accessible language and take account of their normative or political utterances under the conditions of the liberal state. Thus the plea for making a sharp separation between faith and reason is directed against tendencies to overstrain the concept of faith. Religion is thematized as the other of reason.

An analysis of Habermas's separation between the moral and the ethical uses of practical reason seems especially important for an adequate understanding of this distinction (Habermas 1993, pp. 1–17). When they make an ethical-existential use of their reason, human beings express material values which are embedded in, and thus depend upon, their respective lifeworld contexts. Ethical questions are situated at the individual level and are geared to the telos of each individual's life. In the moral domain, by contrast, universal – that is, impartially justified – claims to validity can be raised which are the product of ideal communication processes. Habermas here employs a narrow, formal concept of morality when he emphasizes that, within the moral domain of justification, "[o]nly those norms can claim to be valid that meet (or could meet) with the approval of all affected in their capacity as participants in a practical discourse" (Habermas 1991a, p. 93).

The role of philosophy duly follows from this separation between morality and ethics. It does not take any substantive positions in the ethical domain, but instead confines itself to the role of moderator. Philosophy reconstructs the arguments which derive their support from the ethical worldviews and focuses on the formal (and rational) rules governing the exchange of arguments. However it cannot make a rational decision between competing worldviews.

Religious utterances belong to the ethical use of practical reason and hence to the individual conceptions of the good life which are embedded in the lifeworld. Of course, they also refer to the community and have a high degree of plausibility for the people concerned. Habermas emphasizes, however, that the questions concerning intersubjective relations of recognition and the validity of norms are not ultimately affected by this. Hence philosophy leaves the plausibility of religious worldviews unaffected. The criterion of differentiation between morality and religion as part of ethics is "the universal accessibility of the language and the public accessibility of the reasons admitted into discourse" (Habermas 2007b, p. 381). In morality, therefore, Habermas proceeds from a formal, but ultimately unified reason, whereas in ethics he assumes a plurality of ethical worldviews, which is why universal claims to validity cannot be raised in this domain.

The question is: Can morality and ethics be separated as Habermas proposes? Philosophy has dealt in a variety of ways with the question of the rationality or reasonableness [*Vernünftigkeit*] of the ethical domain. The reconstruction and argumentative justification of ethical worldviews ultimately rest on the assumption that they are cognitively accessible. Many approaches in contemporary debates concerning virtue ethics are also based on a universal concept of the good life for which good arguments can be offered, for example, those developed by Martha Nussbaum. Even though these arguments may not convince all philosophers, it nevertheless does not seem possible to shunt them off into the domain of a merely individually plausible ethics based on a distinction between ethics and morality. The fact that the competition between ethical worldviews cannot be decided in a rational manner is not of itself a sufficient reason to make such a clear separation. On the contrary, ethical worldviews also seem to be cognitively accessible. Concepts of the good life not only represent a resource for individual citizens but they also represent substantive normative concepts for which rational grounds can be adduced. Ultimately this line of reflection also leads us to question Habermas as to whether the separation between morality and ethics rests on too narrow an understanding of religion, which should instead be conceived more broadly, not just for reasons of social theory, but also for ethical reasons.

Remarks in the Philosophy of Religion on the Relation Between Faith and Reason

Habermas's concept of reason is also reflected in the separation between morality and ethics. Although discourse ethics emphasizes the plurality of worldviews, because it assumes that it is possible to reach a rational agreement on validity claims in discourse, it nevertheless implies a strong concept of reason in the sense of a unity of reason. Human beings are capable of reaching an agreement through a hermeneutic procedure and based on a common use of reason. In what follows I will argue that the strong concept of reason should be transformed in such a way that worldviews can also be ascribed a rationality of their own. However, this calls for a new definition of the relation between faith and reason.

To this end, we will first consider Habermas's understanding of reason once again from the perspective of the goal of his argument. The ideal-typical separation between the unity of reason and the plurality of worldviews in Habermas is based on the underlying concern to conceptualize philosophy as formally as possible and to shield it against all "hostile takeovers." As regards the relation between religion and philosophy, this implies that once the "boundary between faith and knowledge becomes porous, and once religious motives force their way into philosophy *under false pretences*, reason loses its foothold and succumbs to irrational effusion" (Habermas 2008, p. 242–3).

Neither at the individual nor at the social level, however, can one make such a clear separation between secular and religious aspects. This is why Thomas Schmidt (2007) develops at the level of the individual "the image of a secular person of faith who exposes his religious convictions to the dissonant surroundings of a pluralist society in a constant reflexive switching between internal and external perspectives" (Habermas 2007b, p. 411). The interconnection between religious and secular arguments which always holds at the individual level is an initial pointer to a reciprocal interrelation between faith and reason. This interrelation also runs through the social level. Secular and religious arguments play an equal and generally also interconnected role within the complex social structure of religious communities. Habermas, on the contrary, seems to want to separate these arguments and assumes that religious citizens make public statements as individuals based on their personal religious choices. Here more importance could be attached to the multidimensional character of social formations, and hence to the interrelation between faith and reason in religious modes of argumentation.[2]

Just as secular and religious arguments cannot be distinguished at the level of individual citizens and within social formations, a sharp distinction cannot be made within the philosophy of religion between faith and reason. Derrida emphasizes for both historical and systematic reasons that "both faith and knowledge are sources of religion," and hence that, although reflection on religion

[2] Underlying this is also a query concerning an excessively sharp distinction between the public and private spheres, as posed, in particular, by feminist scholarship for emancipatory reasons.

44

cannot be conducted within the domain of reason, it can take place on its margins. For Derrida, faith and reason, as intellectual formations, are intrinsically interdependent. Faith, as the thematization of transcendence or experience of the other, gains entry to the domain of reason, and faith – precisely on account of the ambivalence of religions – depends inherently on rational reflection.

Habermas himself draws attention to this fact in two passages of the present lecture, first when he identifies faith and reason from a genealogical perspective as two complementary intellectual formations, and, second, when he assumes that faith can be cognitively disclosed in underlining the necessity of a mutual translation of religious and secular arguments. But how is such a transition possible without also assuming the reasonableness of expressions of faith? Here Habermas himself seems to forge a link between reason and faith through which faith is accorded a rationality of its own, but without assuming a hostile takeover of philosophy by religion.

In order to be able to pursue this thought further, I will propose in conclusion a conception of reason through which the demonstrated interconnection between faith and reason can be conceptualized. A philosopher and theologian whose reflections on faith and reason likewise took place at a time in which religious diversity became socially visible from a "global" perspective, and who responded by reflecting on the concept of reason, is Nicholas of Cusa. If he is read as an epistemologist rather than as a metaphysician, it becomes apparent that he wants to avoid a narrow concept of rationality by means of a relational understanding of knowledge and that at the same time he inquires into the limits of the faculty of knowledge. The possibilities and limits of the human faculty of knowledge are revealed in a paradigmatic way through the question concerning the absolute. Because the absolute transcends all finite oppositions, reason can approach it only by thinking of it as the coincidence of the contradictory oppositions. The preoccupation with religion becomes a matter of *Docta Ignorantia*, with which Nicholas seeks a rational approach to what is located beyond reason (see Inthorn and Reder 2005). In outlining a science of ignorance or non-knowing [*Nichtwissen*], he undertakes a mediation of faith and reason within the tradition of negative theology which is capable of uniting unity and plurality at a fundamental level.[3]

A continuation of this line of thought can be found in Schleiermacher, with whose understanding of religion Habermas likewise deals. Schleiermacher takes his orientation from Nicholas in so far as, for him, the impossibility of a reflexive self-grounding leads to a *Docta Ignorantia* concerning the immediate awareness of self. The experience of the failure of the autonomous self-grounding of reason reveals for him the limits of reason and with this – if we follow the argument of Manfred Frank – the negative signature of human consciousness (Frank 1977). The latter points, in turn, to a transcendent ground which is always prior to consciousness and which can be thematized through a learned ignorance as the whence [*Woher*] of human existence (see Eckert 1987). Applied to religion, Schleiermacher interprets the immediate self-awareness as an absolute feeling of dependency in which the human consciousness of the divine finds expression. Reflection on the foundations of the subject, therefore, reveals not only the limits of an excessively strong conception of reason but also a bridge between faith and reason: religion as a manifestation of the feeling of absolute dependency is not irrational but can be thematized, though never fully grasped, by a reason conscious of its limits.

We can now draw two important conclusions from an account of the relation between faith and reason which follows Nicholas and Schleiermacher. On the one hand, neither thinker makes a sharp distinction between faith

---

[3] A very similar definition of the relation between faith and knowledge can be found in the medieval Islamic tradition, for example in al-Ghazzali.

and reason, but construes the difference instead in a negative-dialectical way as a relation of reciprocal determination. The reason which reflects on its limits runs up against something inaccessible, yet at the same time this inaccessibility can be thematized by reason in the sense of a learned ignorance.

The systematic connection between religion and culture, on the other hand, can be highlighted especially through the confrontation with Schleiermacher. Schleiermacher emphasizes that the feeling of absolute dependency always bears an individual and cultural stamp. The forms of piety in which it finds expression are determined by the respective cultural contexts. For this reason there is neither an original religion [*Urreligion*] behind the feeling of dependency for Schleiermacher, nor can the demonstrated negative-dialectical structure of religion be superseded by a higher synthesis. Because the feeling of absolute dependency always needs some cultural expression, religion and culture constitute inherently interdependent domains.

Habermas highlights Schleiermacher's achievements concerning the mediation between religion and culture and emphasizes that he is the "pacemaker for the consciousness of a post-secular society that accepts the continued existence of religion in an environment that is becoming progressively more secular" (Habermas 2008, p. 242). However, he interprets Schleiermacher's understanding of religion in such a way that, with social integration and the privatization of faith, it is robbed of its inner-worldly explosive power. However, this interrelationship between the secularization, the privatization, and the depoliticization of religion is not a causal one, as is underlined, for example, by the sociologist of religion José Casanova. The privatization of religion, which is correlated in various ways with an institutionalization of religious forms, restricts its social-political relevance only in part and not of necessity.

For this reason Habermas's interpretation of Schleiermacher holds only with qualification. By privileging

Schleiermacher's understanding of religion over Kant's, by contrast, above all the connection between religion and morality to which Habermas accords priority could be revoked and the interrelation between religion highlighted instead.

Moreover, reflection on the connection between religion and culture in the context of global networks has certain advantages for an interreligious dialogue. If we follow Nicholas and Schleiermacher in emphasizing the respective limits of and interrelations between faith and reason and, as regards religion, approach the absolute in a way which is critical of reason in the sense of a *Docta Ignorantia*, then the boundaries of religious knowledge can always also be highlighted within the global context, as Nicholas demonstrates in an exemplary way in *De pace fidei*. An interreligious dialogue, which following Nicholas and Schleiermacher can be understood in precisely Habermas's sense as a call to engage in discourse, is easier to conduct in the light of such a negative-dialectical understanding of religion than if the truth claims of religions are banished into the domain of individual worldviews.

Outlook

Deliberative democracy aims at a constitutionally guaranteed integration of all citizens into political negotiation processes under the premises of liberal thought. This concern seems especially important and reasonable in the light of global challenges. What is at issue is making it possible for all people throughout the world to participate actively (and not merely passively or as victims) in the political process. The challenge for political philosophy is to stimulate this process through arguments and models and to respond constructively to new developments. From this perspective, Habermas's engagement with religion represents an important stimulus for present-day reflection on global processes.

In his reflections on religion he focuses on worldviews, and thereby attaches greater importance to the embeddedness of discourses in cultural contexts, as communitarians demand. However, in doing so he remains within the familiar framework of discourse ethics. In the sense in which philosophy is today called upon to take positions on social questions, Habermas points to the moral potential which resides in religions. Thus if, to put it graphically, participants in social discourses today point to the philosopher and interrogate him concerning ethical orientations, the philosopher (Habermas) points in turn to religions which could offer resources for clarifying normative questions. The major advantage of this conception is its formal modesty: it does not advocate substantive normative positions and it thus represents a paradigmatic expression of the liberal, democratic constitutional state. The disadvantage is that religions ultimately remain within the sphere of the ethical and can thus be ascribed only a conditional rationality of their own. Even from the perspective of deliberative democracy, however, religions cannot be thematized only in terms of the "awareness of what is missing," but must also be thematized as a substantive, rationally reconstructible element of ethical and cultural reflection on society.[4]

Reflections within ethics and the philosophy of religion have shown that one can reasonably go beyond Habermas's position even under the premises of liberal thought. Religious arguments could have even greater impact in the public arena in the light of a broad understanding of reason (which does not distinguish it sharply from faith). Important for this is an understanding of reason which takes into account both the limits of reason and of the reasonableness or rationality of faith in the sense of a *Docta Ignorantia*. From the perspective of social theory, of course,

[4] Compare Maeve Cooke's attempt to draw upon the theory of deliberative democracy to talk not only in terms of a post-secular society but also of a post-secular state (see Cooke 2007).

the intelligibility of the arguments and the recognition of plurality remain the central formal criterion; but the proposed view would not question this either. In the controversy with Rawls's narrower understanding of religion, Habermas himself stresses that the vitality of the liberal state rests on its multivocal character and that citizens owe one another reasons for their positions in the sense of reciprocal perspective-taking. Precisely this multivocal character and the recognition of the reasonableness of these expressions could be accorded greater importance, especially from a global perspective, not least in order to facilitate a constructive interreligious and intercultural discourse concerning the political organization of world society.

5
Postmetaphysical Reason and Religion

FRIEDO RICKEN, S. J.

How, Habermas asks, should modern reason, which has turned its back on metaphysics, understand itself in relation to religion? His answer involves an expectation of both sides: modern reason should not understand itself in a secularistic sense (I), and theology must seriously engage with postmetaphysical thinking (II).

I

The first demand results from the deficiencies of secular reason. Habermas refers to the "defeatism concerning reason" which we encounter in an Enlightenment radicalized by postmodernism and in a naturalism based on naive faith in science; however, postmetaphysical thinking can cope with this. More serious, Habermas thinks, is the deficient motivation of practical reason. It fails to fulfill its own vocation when it no longer has the power to awaken "in the minds of secular subjects an awareness of the violations of solidarity throughout the world." Habermas asks whether "a different perspective on the genealogy of reason" could "rescue postmetaphysical thinking from this dilemma." Philosophy and religion, he argues, have a shared origin; they represent two "complementary intellectual formations." "Complementary" means that they

51

supplement each other and depend upon each other. The religious traditions constitute a reservoir on which a reason which is willing to learn draws, and secular reason has the ability and the task to translate contents of the religious traditions into its own language.

An example of such a translation can be found in Habermas's address on receiving the Peace Prize of the German Book Trade. Habermas translates Genesis 1.27 into a contribution to the debate concerning the treatment of embryos which "can speak even to the religiously tone-deaf." Let me try to reconstruct his train of thought. The biblical verse reads as follows: "So God created humankind in his image, in the image of God he created them." It contains two assertions: human beings bear a likeness to God and are creatures of God. Philosophy expresses the fact that human beings bear a likeness to God as follows: they are beings endowed with and bound by freedom. Because every human being is an image of God, all human beings are equally free. That human beings are God's creatures can be translated into a negative assertion concerning the relation between human beings: human beings do not owe their natural essence to other human beings. Anyone who determines "*at his own discretion*, the natural essence of another human being" (Habermas 2003, p. 115) transgresses, in the language of the Bible, the boundary between creature and creator. This can be expressed as follows in philosophical language: he fails to respect the reciprocal relation among human beings implied by equal freedom; by determining the natural essence of the other at his own discretion, he violates the principle of equal freedom.

But how can a changed perspective on the genealogy of reason make good the motivational deficit of practical reason and awaken a consciousness of the worldwide violation of solidarity? The return to the prehistory of the emergence of reason can be understood as the reverse process to that of translation. Translation leads to abstract concepts; the study of genealogy leads us back to the lifeworld context, to the anthropological phenomena, on which this abstraction is based. Religions perform a maieutic function in the sense that they enable us to see these phenomena, force us to confront them, and trigger our responses. Thus the abstract concept of transcendental freedom, for example, has its origins in the concept of guilt, and what guilt means in lifeworld terms and how we experience it are shown by the corresponding religious narratives. Only through the encounter with the latter, therefore, can "an awareness of what is missing, of what cries out to heaven" be awakened and kept awake.

Faith and reason, "together with their traditions based respectively in Jerusalem and Athens," belong "to the history of the origins of secular reason." The example of Kant shows how these two currents in the western tradition flow together in the Enlightenment concept of reason. Mosaic monotheism is a religion marked by an all-encompassing trust. For Plato, the highest object of reason is the Form of the Good; reason in its most developed form leads to a comprehensive sense of the whole. Habermas quotes Adorno's dictum that the secret of the Kantian philosophy is "the unthinkability of despair" (Habermas 2008, p. 221). Kant links Athens and Jerusalem in his concept of rational faith. "Faith (simply so-called) is trust in the attainment of an aim the promotion of which is a duty but the possibility of the realization of which it is not possible for us to have insight into" (*Critique of the Power of Judgement*, 5:472, p. 317).

II

Theology, according to the demand which Habermas addresses to religion, must engage seriously with post-metaphysical thinking. Habermas criticizes Pope Benedict XVI for rejecting this demand in his Regensburg lecture. The Pope, according to Habermas, gave the old controversy over the Hellenization and de-Hellenization of

Christianity an interpretation "which is unexpectedly critical of modernity" and thereby gave a negative answer to
the question "of whether Christian theology must wrestle
with the challenges of modern, postmetaphysical reason.
The Pope appeals to the synthesis of Greek metaphysics
and biblical faith forged in the tradition extending
from Augustine to Thomas, and he implicitly denies that
there are good reasons for the polarization between faith
and knowledge which became an empirical feature of
European modernity."

Before dealing with this controversy, I would like to
highlight the concern which Benedict XVI and Habermas
share. Both take a stand against a narrow scientistic concept
of reason. Habermas speaks of a "naturalism based on
naive faith in science" and Benedict XVI (see Benedict
XVI 2006) objects to a "modern concept of reason" which
is based "on a synthesis between Platonism (Cartesianism)
and empiricism, a synthesis confirmed by the success of
technology"; his concern is to "[broaden] our concept of
reason and its application"; he wants "to disclose [the] vast
horizons" of reason. Both of them point to religious traditions as resources of reason. Benedict XVI: "For philosophy . . . listening to the great experiences and insights of
the religious traditions of humanity, and those of the
Christian faith in particular, is a source of knowledge, and
to ignore it would be an unacceptable restriction of our
listening and responding" (Benedict XVI 2006). Habermas: The theological self-understanding looms over our
modernity "as the most awkward element from its past,"
and it must preserve its awkwardness because "[p]hiloso-
phy can draw *rational* sustenance from the religious
heritage only as long as the source of revelation that ortho-
doxy counterposes to philosophy remains a cognitively
unacceptable imposition for the latter" (Habermas 2008,
p. 242).

A first difference of opinion between Habermas and
Benedict XVI arises over the concept of Hellenization.
Habermas understands by this "the synthesis of faith and

knowledge forged in the tradition extending from Augustine to Thomas" and he bases his criticism of Benedict XVI on this concept. By contrast, Benedict XVI means an inner-biblical process which reaches its conclusion in the prologue to the Gospel of St John. In the first sentence of the prologue, John "spoke the final word on the biblical concept of God, and in this word all the often toilsome and tortuous threads of biblical faith find their culmination and synthesis. In the beginning was the *logos*, and the *logos* is God, says the Evangelist." As phases in this development, the Pope identifies the revelation of the name of God from the burning bush (Exodus 3:14), the wisdom literature, and the Greek translation of the Old Testament, the Septuagint. Thus the encounter between Athens and Jerusalem takes place already within the Bible. De-Hellenization, therefore, cannot be understood as a return to scripture; rather it would unavoidably entail the dissolution of the unity of the Bible.

The second difference of opinion concerns the modern concept of reason. According to the Pope, the first wave of de-Hellenization was linked with the main concern of the sixteenth-century Reformation; faith had to be liberated from metaphysics in order to recover its true self. "When Kant stated that he needed to set thinking aside in order to make room for faith, he carried this program forward with a radicalism that the Reformers could never have foreseen. He thus anchored faith exclusively in practical reason, denying it access to reality as a whole." Behind the nineteenth and twentieth-century liberal theology, of which Adolf von Harnack is the primary representative and which for Benedict XVI represents a second wave of de-Hellenization, lies "the modern self-limitation of reason, classically expressed in Kant's 'Critiques', but in the meantime further radicalized by the impact of the natural sciences. This modern concept of reason is based . . . on a synthesis between Platonism (Cartesianism) and empiricism, a synthesis confirmed by the success of technology" (Benedict XVI 2006).

55

Neither of these two quotations even begins to do justice to the Kantian concept of reason. Reason enquires into the unconditioned; the critique of theoretical reason leaves this question open and practical philosophy, taking as its point of departure the apodictic law of practical reason, answers it through rational faith. It is difficult to understand how Kant can be depicted as the father of a scientistic-naturalistic worldview. His hypothesis of the primacy of practical reason represents a resolute rejection of naturalism; it states that the primary interest of reason consists in our understanding of ourselves as free, morally acting beings. Habermas rightly objects to Benedict XVI's interpretation of Kant that "Kant's transcendental turn leads not only to a critique of the proofs of God's existence but also to the concept of autonomy which first made possible our modern European understanding of law and democracy."

Which concept of reason does Habermas contrast with this? The demand that theology should engage seriously with postmetaphysical thinking and that Christian theology must "wrestle with the challenges of modern, post-metaphysical reason" can be understood only in the light of an explanation of how this postmetaphysical reason should be conceived and of what it is capable.

A postmetaphysical reason is a reason which has broken "with metaphysical constructions of the totality of nature and history." Not much more is left for philosophy "than the general competences of knowing, speaking, and acting subjects." This minimalistic sounding definition must be supplemented by the capabilities and functions which Habermas ascribes to postmetaphysical reason in the present text. It can defend itself against a postmodern and scientistic-naturalistic defeatism concerning reason; thus it is not a scientistic, but a critical reason which is able to reflect on its possibilities and limitations and its various forms. As regards religions, it is a "receptive" [lernbereit] reason. With this it also faces the question concerning the relation between faith and knowledge, for receptiveness means that it confronts the religions with an "anticipation of completeness" (Gadamer: *Vorgriff der Vollkommenheit*) and in this sense with an act of faith.

Postmetaphysical reason has the ability to translate semantic contents of religions into universally accessible discourses, though it must be emphasized in this context that it is always a matter of individual contents which do not extend as far as the core of faith as a whole. "Providing an apology for faith employing philosophical means is not a task for philosophy proper. At best, philosophy *circumscribes* the opaque core of religious experience when it reflects on the specific character of religious language and on the intrinsic meaning of faith" (Habermas 2008, p. 143).

This translation has a traditional counterpart. The doctrine of the natural moral law is a translation of parts of the Judeo-Christian moral teaching into the language of philosophy; Thomas Aquinas's "five ways" seek to ensure the possibility of a scientific development of revelation through a philosophical proof of God's existence. This correlation raises a question concerning Habermas's program of translation. For its translation, the tradition made use of Stoic and Aristotelian moral philosophy, Aristotelian epistemology, and Aristotelian metaphysics. What means does postmetaphysical reason have at its disposal if it is to perform a translation rather than an assimilation, a translation in which parts of the religious traditions are transposed into another language without detriment to their semantic content? Kant describes his method of translation as follows: he wants "to hold fragments of this revelation, as a historical system, up to moral concepts" (*Religion within the Boundaries of Mere Reason* 6:12, p. 40). Does the moral consciousness which has not been undermined by scientism supply postmetaphysical reason with the necessary categories for its task of translation?

Habermas demands that Christian theology "must wrestle with the challenges of modern, postmetaphysical reason." This implies two tasks and leads back to the discussion concerning the Hellenization of Christianity.

Christian theology must first make an authoritative contribution to the process of translation prescribed by postmetaphysical reason. It must in this way make available
to a secular society "the unexhausted force" [*das Unabgegoltene*] in its tradition. In so doing it merely pursues
further a concern which has occupied it since the second-
century apologists and to which natural theology and the
doctrine of the natural moral law should lend support;
what has changed, however, is the language into which
it must be translated. The valid concern of the critics of
Hellenization is that this must not be a matter of replac-
ing the biblical message of salvation with a middle- or
neo-Platonic metaphysics, and that always only certain
marginal areas, the *praeambula fidei*, are accessible to this
translation, never the core and the whole.

Second, theology must ensure that the religious tradition retains its awkwardness and that the Christian revelation remains a "cognitively unacceptable imposition" for
secular thought. Here a different concept of Hellenization
and its valid concern comes into play. The Judeo-Christian
message of salvation was already reflected in the Bible
with the help of concepts derived from Greek philosophy.
Greek philosophy served as an instrument for interpreting
the biblical message, but it did not take the place of the
biblical message. The instrumentarium of Greek philosophy was used instead to throw light upon the true concern
of the biblical message and to guard against misinterpreta-
tions. In this reflection, through which the community
seeks to grasp the Judeo-Christian message of salvation in
its entirety – in this systematic hermeneutics of the biblical
message – the question arises of which conceptual instrumentarium is suited to this task. For anyone who wishes
to replace the Greek concepts, as formulated, for example,
by Nicaea and Chalcedon, with different ones must prove
that these other concepts capture the awkwardness and
provocativeness of the biblical message as well as do the
concepts of Greek metaphysics.

6
A Dialogue in Which There Can Only Be Winners

JOSEF SCHMIDT, S. J.

In his contribution, Jürgen Habermas makes a plea for a fair dialogue between enlightened reason and religious faith, for "it makes a difference whether we speak with one another or merely about one another." Among his well-known merits is to have worked out the dialogical dimension of reason in a convincing manner. Reason, according to Habermas, is essentially communicative action in which one's own reflection is also embedded, and, as such, it constitutes the single unifying and binding reason. If someone confirms it by, for example, making an assertion for herself or towards others, then she presupposes that this assertion is also justifiable, that is, that anyone who has the corresponding insight will agree with it. Force and manipulation cannot be reconciled with such a claim, for insight can only develop freely and its justification can achieve its goal only in an insight which is arrived at freely. Assertion aims at truth and claims truth for itself. But truth is valid for all beings who are capable of comprehending the truth. This universally binding reference to truth opens up the horizon of an inclusive community to which all those belong who are capable of understanding, even incipiently, that something "is" and "is valid." Because of this ability, which must always be assumed or anticipated, they all represent possible conversational partners in a free dialogue whose outcome remains open.

Among the necessary presuppositions of such communication Habermas numbers: the use of an understandable
language (1), the reference to an in principle universally
accessible and binding truth (2), one's own truthfulness
and the assumption that others are truthful (3), and the
recognition of the norms posited by the reciprocity of this
reasonable action (4). Although it is empirically possible
to contest these assumptions, it is impossible in a "performative" sense – in other words, it is contradictory because,
in the act of contesting them, one unavoidably assumes
them.

This opens up a space of reflection which transforms
human beings into equal partners. All questions concerned
with truth and rightness, especially those of common
concern, whether in everyday life, in science, or in the
organization of social interaction, can be negotiated within
this reflexive framework, but at the same time are subject
to its orienting standards. Proposals, attempts at answers,
and a whole variety of options may and ought to find
expression, but they have to prove their worth within this
communicative framework. In other words, they must not
violate its performative presuppositions and only if they
cohere with the latter and at the same time make them
explicit are they suited to filling its universal form with
life and content. The absolute validity of this form becomes
apparent in the nonarbitrariness of truth and morality.
What is the source of this nonarbitrariness, where does the
categorical acquire its character as a demand? It is the
result of the nonarbitrary character of the aforementioned
communicative framework. The latter binds unconditionally. Its unconditionality authorizes it to do so because this
framework represents the irreducible circle within which
reason turns and enjoys its autonomy [*über sich verfügt*].
Because its validity cannot come from outside – since
to adopt an external standpoint would be to succumb
to the performative contradiction which merely confirms
this validity – it is absolutely unconditional. It is not
a vicious circle. For any such circle is erroneous and

must be avoided. In other words, it is avoidable because it proceeds from an assumption that need not apply. However, this non-applicability is inconceivable within the performative circle – or, to be more precise, it is unthinkable because unrealizable, and it is just this which constitutes the unconditional character of the circle. If a demand follows from this circle, then it is ineluctable, that is, it is not merely a hypothetical but a categorical, unconditional demand. It is, however, subject to differentiation, and thus there follow the normative conditions which Habermas outlines – the basic demands of the morality of justice, of the respect for the freedom and dignity of human beings (my own and that of others), and of the even-handed treatment of the claims to freedom of all concerned. All of the concrete claims and options of those concerned must be examined and judged in the light of this unconditionality. They should be tolerated or affirmed in accordance with its standards or they must be rejected if they conflict with the latter. In this way, reason specifies a "procedure" (Habermas) for testing claims of whatever kind. Yet reason is not merely formal but, in its characteristic unconditionality, has substantive import, for its form contains the foundation of freedom and morality and the concrete development of its universal (thus still formal) content must take its orientation from itself and is always subject to its own critical verification.

But what happens when reason, thus understood, encounters religious faith and enters into a dialogue with it? A fair dialogue is characterized by the fact that the partners take each other seriously, and hence do not speak about one another but with one another. But this requires that one should not assume from the outset that the other's convictions are irrational, so that one does not regard them as even capable of being true nor, as a consequence, as worthy of discussion, but merely as in need of explanation (why do they say that?). In such a case, dialogue would come to an abrupt end. The partner would not feel herself taken seriously in what she thinks is essential. If a dialogue

worthy of the name is to take place, the discussion partners must assume that their respective convictions are in
essence intelligible, not that they are necessarily true but
that they are worthy of discussion as regards their truth in
a fair exchange of arguments. This is what Habermas is
getting at when he repeatedly emphasizes that what is at
stake in the discourse with religion is the "not yet exhausted
intelligible potentials" of its utterances. For the religious
person, this means, of course, that she must understand
her own statements in such a way that they can be introduced into such a conversation. If she wants to be taken
seriously, she must present her faith accordingly as worthy
of discussion. Otherwise she cannot be taken seriously
(or does not even want to be taken seriously in this way);
but then she may not demand (vociferously) to be taken
seriously either.

In what follows I will attempt to qualify the religious
partner for this conversation, that is, to present her conception in a correspondingly intelligible form, and hence
one worthy of discussion, yet without truncating its substance but in order to clarify its distinctive meaning. This
was the concern of Christian theology from the beginning,
namely, to understand and communicate the talk of
the "theos" as "logos," and this as logos of the "Word" of
God and of itself, and at the same time of the shared
"logos" which unites human beings, which is "the light,"
which "enlightens everyone [!]" (John 1.9). Such a self-
presentation belongs to the essence of the Christian
message (1 Peter 3.15). For this reason, I will draw in what
follows on certain basic articles of the Judeo-Christian
faith (which may also hold in a similar way for Islam, and
thus constitute central tenets of the Abrahamic religions).
This seems to me to be the only way to conduct a serious
dialogue between enlightened reason and religious faith
(whatever its provenance).

The central content of the biblical faith is God himself.
This is expressed by the first commandment of Mount
Sinai. God alone! No other gods! The orientation to the

single infinite God makes human beings capable of the infinite, and this constitutes their freedom. They are no longer subjected to any limited powers of any kind; they are not "enslaved" to them. God reveals himself to human beings accordingly as a liberator: "I am the Lord your God, who brought you out of the land of Egypt, out of the house of slavery; you shall have no other gods before me" (Deuteronomy 5.6–7). The worship of the one God liberates human beings from all possible idols and earthly powers. Thus their freedom depends on this capacity for transcendence. But only if their transcending has a corresponding "wherefore" are they capable of this. Only that which is perfectly infinite, and in this sense absolutely singular, grants human beings the possibility of this act of radical transcendence. Thus this goal must also be conceived accordingly, namely as nonidentical with anything that is visible, objectifiable, and limited. This is the source of the prohibition on images: "You shall not make for yourself an idol, whether in the form of anything that is in heaven above, or that is on the earth beneath, or that is in the water under the earth. You shall not bow down to them or worship them" (Deuteronomy 5.8–9). Yet this God can be named. He is not entirely inaccessible. In his peculiar distance he is simultaneously close to human beings. He has opened himself up to communication and has given himself a name. Experiencing him as God, thinking about, talking about and with him – all of this proceeds from him and are not merely a human projection, a conversation among ourselves.

This name, "Yahweh" (whose precise meaning is "I am who I am") or "Elohim," "God" (because, in the light of God's uniqueness, this term lost its meaning as a generic concept and became a proper name), is the designation under which the one thus designated presents himself (Exodus 3.13ff.). And this name of his – that is, the speech addressed to him and about him – must not be misused or instrumentalized. "You shall not make wrongful use of the name of the Lord your God" (Deuteronomy 5.11).

God is not a means for some other purpose, but an end in himself and for his own sake. Thus he is unconditionally good and hence the foundation and goal of all goodness. Only through him does striving have meaning, and only in him does it come to rest. However, human beings have to remind themselves of this rest repeatedly and to embrace it – hence, the obligation to keep the sabbath. Although work is important, it is not everything. Human beings must be protected against becoming enslaved to the idol work. Hence the necessity of a social order in which this rest from work has its place: "Observe the sabbath day and keep it holy, as the Lord your God commanded you. Six days you shall labor and do all your work. But the seventh day is a sabbath to the Lord your God; you shall not do any work – you, or your son or your daughter, or your male or female slave, or your ox or your donkey, or any of your livestock, or the resident alien in your towns, so that your male and female slave may rest as well as you. Remember that you were a slave in the land of Egypt, and the Lord your God brought you out from there with a mighty hand" (Deuteronomy 5.12ff.). The contemplation of the self-sufficient God is not contingent on utility of any kind, and thus human beings exist for themselves only insofar as they exist for God. Our fellow human beings must be viewed in the same way, so that the command to observe the sabbath provides a suitable transition to the commandments which concern our fellow human beings: to honor our parents, not to commit adultery, not to commit murder, to steal, or to lie, and not to covet what belongs to others, be it their wife or their goods (Deuteronomy 5.16ff.).

The turning towards God makes human beings human and founds their freedom. In orienting themselves towards him, God represents himself in them. He appears in their countenance in that he makes them capable of openness towards themselves, thus endowing them with intelligence and freedom. This is why it is said that God made human beings in his "image" (Genesis 1.26), thereby lending them their dignity and inviolability. The prohibition on murder is explicitly justified in terms of this likeness to God (Genesis 9.6). But this inviolability also provides genuine protection just because it is a law which is not made by human beings. Anyone who violates human dignity not only has human law and its sanctions against her but also God himself, the absolutely unconditioned, with all the consequences of self-contradiction and self-destruction. Moreover, this contradiction goes so far that the preservation of the human dignity is even impervious to bodily destruction, so that the murderer is condemned to impotence. This certainty of ultimate security in God developed and was clarified in the later strata of the Bible into the hope in God beyond this life. This faith is strikingly depicted in a story from the time of the Maccabean revolt against the tyranny of the Seleucid ruler Antiochus Epiphanes, who, in the grip of a totalitarian Hellenizing mania, called upon the Jews to renounce their faith and thus to violate their conscience. A mother was forced to look on as her steadfast sons were executed one after the other. To the youngest she herself offered words of encouragement: "I beg you, my child, to look at the heaven and the earth and see everything that is in them, and recognize that God did not make them out of things that existed. And in the same way the human race came into being. Do not fear this butcher, but prove worthy of your brothers. Accept death, so that in God's mercy I may get you back again along with your brothers" (2 Maccabees 7.28f.) Standing before the void, human beings can hope only in him who wields power even over the void. In him they can have knowledge of ultimate security, come what may. For of him who demands so much of them, raises them up, and shows such interest in them, of such a God human beings can say: "If God is for us, who is against us?" (Romans 8.31).

All of this follows from the first commandment: God alone! He alone, who exists absolutely in and for himself, is also unconditionally good and, in this unconditionality, is the foundation of all morality, but also of all hopes associated with its unconditional demands. The result is a coherent order of things which can withstand the wisdom of the world. Moses proudly declares: "[F]or this will show your wisdom and discernment to the peoples, who, when they hear all these statutes, will say, 'Surely this great nation is a wise and discerning people!' For what other great nation has a god so near to it as the Lord our God is whenever we call to him? And what other great nation has statutes and ordinances as just as this entire law that I am setting before you today?" (Deuteronomy 4.6ff.). Being rational means that that which cannot be surpassed is closer to human beings than anything else; or in philosophical terms, the absolutely unconditioned is the innermost a priori. Thus the orientation to the infinite, unique God grounds human freedom and autonomy and the inclusiveness of the human mind and the universality of human morality.

What can it mean that enlightened reason enters into a dialogue with such a faith? Faith has nothing to fear from reason, nor will reason have to shrink back from faith as something irrational. Nevertheless, the "conversation," according to Habermas, is characterized by "two presuppositions": "The religious side must accept the authority of 'natural' reason in both its theoretical and practical respects, that is, both the fallible results of the institutionalized sciences and the basic principles of universalistic egalitarianism in law and morality. Conversely, the secular side must take religion seriously as an intellectual formation; it may not set itself up as the judge concerning the potentially rational content of religious traditions, even though in the end it can accept as reasonable only what it can translate into its own, in principle universally accessible, discourses" (Habermas 2007a). Neither side need fear such a conversation or regard it as hopeless – on the contrary. Each side can see it as an opportunity, and can even expose itself to criticism to its own advantage. Secular reason must face the question of where it has drawn its own rational boundaries too hastily, so that the latter do not match its real scope. The person of faith must expect to have her attention drawn to many inessential elements based on superstition or ideology from which she must free herself in the light of reason and in order to enhance the persuasiveness of her message.

Habermas has clarified the essential presuppositions of such a discourse. He has rescued reason from a scientistic narrowing and has recovered the space within which its genuine questions can be adequately addressed, its own space as the ineluctable, uniting, and binding practice of rational communication. In his Peace Prize speech, he states: "The scientistic belief in a science which will one day not only supplement, but *replace* the self-understanding of actors as persons by an objectivating self-description, is not science but bad philosophy" (Habermas 2003, p. 108). Human beings always have to deal with "themselves" and not with objects, and thus they cannot wish to make themselves into mere objects without committing a performative contradiction. This "self" locates them from the outset in the inclusive reflexive space within which the questions concerning truth, goodness, and a regulation of social life can be meaningfully posed in the first place, simply because these questions aim at an, in principle, mutual understanding among human beings and they cannot be addressed apart from the orientation to this goal. All answers proposed in this context must be judged scientifically and are thus "fallible." However the kind of fallibility which takes the empirical sciences as its model is not the primary or the key element in addressing the foundational questions which arise, but the kind which belongs to a reflexive mode of argumentation which exposes itself to critique.

In his Peace Prize speech, Habermas enters into a dialogue with religious faith and pays tribute to its central assertions as "important resources of meaning" from which "secular society" should not "cut itself off" (Habermas 2003, p. 109). He refers to the central articles of faith mentioned above, to belief in God, to human beings' likeness to God, and to the salvation of human beings from death. Regarding the treatment of human embryos, the doctrine of human beings as created in God's likeness attracts Habermas's attention: "Regarding his origin, he cannot be God's equal. This *creatural nature* of the likeness expresses an intuition which in the present context may even speak to those who are tone-deaf to religious connotations. Hegel had a feeling for this difference between divine 'creation' and mere 'coming from' God. God remains a 'God of free men' only as long as we do not level out the absolute difference that exists between the creator and the creature. Only then, the fact that God gives form to human life does not imply a determination interfering with man's self-determination" (Habermas 2003, pp. 114–15) (translation amended). In a striking passage from the speech, he addresses the third topic: "What is even more disconcerting is the irreversibility of *past* suffering – the injustice inflicted on innocent people who were abused, debased, and murdered, reaching far beyond any extent of reparation within human power. The lost hope for resurrection is keenly felt as a void . . . Both, the true impulse and its impotence, were prolonged after the holocaust by the practice, as necessary as it was hopeless, of 'coming to terms with the past' (Adorno). As it happens, this is precisely what is made apparent by the rising lament over the inappropriateness of this practice. In moments like these, the irreligious sons and daughters of modernity seem to believe that they owe more one another, and themselves need more, than what is accessible to them in translation of religious traditions – as if the semantic potential of the latter was not yet exhausted" (Habermas 2003, pp. 110–11) (translation amended).

This acknowledgment of essential contents of religion initiates a dialogue between religion and secular reason worthy of this name. If one turns one's gaze from these contents to reason as Habermas develops it, religious faith can regard itself as justified and encouraged to introduce its concerns into the dialogue as something intelligible and universally accessible. As regards the approach to the discussion of the idea of God, what is specific to the concept of God will be rationally represented to faith in the unavoidable reflexive circle of reason, namely the absolutely unconditioned to which we human beings are subordinated, even as it endows us with the capacity for intellectual independence and autonomy. For from it alone must the unavoidable obligation to truth and goodness, and the ability to comprehend this, be understood and justified. With this unconditionality is also given the absolute end in itself, God as end in himself, who is present in us and who, as the norm and goal of our striving, constitutes our self-realization. It is he who demands our unconditional respect wherever he appears, in ourselves or in any of our fellow human beings.

Religion has absolutely no reason to fear the dialogue with enlightened reason. For this dialogue enables it to recognize that, far from being alien to it, this reason belongs to its own logos. The dialogue brings religion closer to itself and makes it confident of itself. Thus encouraged, it will also more willingly accept the standards of communicative reason (highlighted by Habermas) for resolving controversial issues in a predominantly secular world. Yet it will also pursue the dialogue self-confidently from its own side. Thus, regarding the reflexive circle of reason, it will ask whether it is sufficient to describe its ineluctable character in terms of "unavoidability" and simply to insist on a "postmetaphysical standpoint." There are undoubtedly good reasons for leaving open the metaphysical interpretation of this circle in our pluralistic world. It avoids a linkage between morality and a particular metaphysics, such that someone could say, for example, "since I do not share such and such a comprehensive view, the requirements of morality do not hold for me either." This is why Kant already spoke of a "fact of reason," though this is actually inconsistent with his thought. Today, too, morality as such a "fact" is much more open to consensus than in connection with a specific comprehensive view. However, we must be allowed to ask whether this "unavoidability" is understood in the sense of an openness for a metaphysical explanation which can then be worked out in discourse or whether it is already understood definitively as an (albeit higher form of) facticity, and hence as a form of metaphysics whose meaning can ultimately be explicated in naturalistic terms. For an openness in the sense that the alternatives are equally valid cannot exist. With the reflexive justification, the admission of an (if only possibly) merely factual explanation is excluded in principle. Thus it must reside in something beyond the factual. Then the question concerning the metaphysical constitution of this supra-factual reality cannot be rejected, however, and faith can recognize in this the point of departure for the enduring discussion-worthiness of the idea of God.

The few indications presented here by no means signal the end of this critical dialogue. Their goal was to show only how exciting and fruitful it remains, and specifically as a dialogue in which we do not speak "about one another but with one another" and in which both sides can recognize that they are taken seriously in their core convictions. Both sides can acknowledge the incompleteness of their respective paths, without this necessarily becoming for them an objection against the robustness of their shared reason. This incompleteness is familiar to the person of faith. For, given the world as it is, faith in a God who takes an interest in us human beings, who "intends" us and who gives us hope where all hope seems to be exhausted, will always remain "nonconformist" and will always be a question and a challenge for the person of faith herself. This is what constitutes the "strangeness" of faith for all of us, and Habermas rightly insists on it. Only in the exercise and at the risk of the most personal responsibility can faith persist as this "paradox" (that is, "against" the "doxa" and in opposition to everything which "seems" to be) and can it as a cousequence find its proof and confirmation only in the credible testimony of one's own life. However, the person of faith can, in turn, learn this very connection with the exercise of freedom from a communicative reason which understands itself as essentially "pragmatic" and in the process can come to recognize herself as one with it.

7
A Reply

JÜRGEN HABERMAS

In the mid-1970s, when the academic climate in Munich was not exactly sympathetic to someone like me, the Jesuits invited me to give a lecture on questions concerning discourse ethics. Recalling this unorthodox and lively discussion, last year I gratefully accepted a further invitation to give a lecture at the Jesuit university. At the university in Kaulbachstrasse I had no reason to fear false embraces. I would like to show my appreciation for that pleasant evening, and above all for the perceptive comments, reservations, and objections, with a brief reply. Once we open ourselves to a dialogue we become caught up in its embrace. I will discuss the contributions in the order in which they were presented. The length of the replies is, of course, in no way a reflection of different assessments of the value of the contributions. Rather, they challenge me to make more or less elaborate responses.

(1) Norbert Brieskorn's question of who is "missing" what and in what sense requires me first to make good a reference which I originally neglected to make. When the formula the "awareness of what is missing" first occurred to me I was still under the influence of reading Johann Baptist Metz's impressive book, *Memoria passionis* (2006), which I should have cited in this context. Both Metz and I draw inspiration, albeit in different ways, from the

heritage of Adorno's thought. This may explain why this formulation struck me as so obvious that it did not need an explicit reference. The religious topos of the inverted and doomed world has been made profane and stripped of its eschatological content in the course of its long peregrination through the works of Schelling, Hegel, and the Young Hegelians. It was finally superseded by the concept of alienation and led at times in the Marxist tradition to the diagnosis of "contentment in alienation." This refers to social pathologies which do not leave behind so much as the critical spur of an awareness of the disorder. Now "alienation" remains a universal anthropological concept and has such strong connotations that it has in the meantime disappeared almost entirely from sociological discourse. However, the phenomena themselves do not automatically disappear with the disappearance of the appropriate means of describing them. Without the normatively imbued description and self-description of "distorted" social relations which violate basic interests, an awareness of "what is missing" cannot arise either. The affirmative tenor of classical ethics lost its relevance long ago. Contemporary philosophy lacks Benjaminian words which go beyond mere cultural criticism.

Violations of universally accepted norms of justice can be more easily established, and denounced with good reasons, than can pathological distortions of forms of life. The moral sensitivity to the unjust distribution of life opportunities has by no means diminished in societies of our type. The sensitivity to social injustice extends not only to the marginalization of groups, the disenfranchisement of social strata, and the dilapidation of regions within one's own country, but also to the more drastic misery on other continents. However, these perceptions and reactions in no way affect the trends towards a breakdown in solidarity in different sectors of society. This increases all the more inexorably the deeper the imperatives of the market, in the guise of cost–benefit analyses or competition to perform, permeate ever more spheres of life and force individuals to adopt an objectivizing standpoint in their dealings with one another. At the level of elementary interactions, a gap seems to be opening up between a prickly moral consciousness and the impotence in the face of the structurally imposed switch to strategic conduct. This makes the withdrawal into the private domain and the repression of awkward cognitive dissonances all the more understandable.

Trends towards the breakdown of solidarity are also disquieting when seen against the background of a scenario which does not merely call for maintaining the political status quo but for the political regulation of an emerging multicultural world society. Only in this way can the manifest risks accompanying the transition from the national to the postnational constellation be dispelled. The most influential governments, however, who remain the most important political actors on this stage, persist undaunted in their social Darwinist power games – even more so since the catastrophe of 9/11 and the reaction to it. Not only is the political will to work towards the institutions and procedures of a reformed global order missing, but even the aspiration to a pacified global domestic politics. I suspect that nothing will change in the parameters of public discussion and in the decisions of the politically empowered actors without the emergence of a social movement which fosters a complete shift in political mentality. The tendencies towards a breakdown in solidarity in everyday life do not exactly render such a mobilization within western civil societies probable.

If we now switch our level of observation and examine, from a philosophical perspective, the resources generated by a cultural modernity which draws on its own sources, we encounter, among other things, the oft-mentioned motivational weaknesses of a rational morality, though these are counterbalanced by positive law within the boundaries of the constitutional state. Rational morality sharpens our faculty of judgment for the violation of individual claims and individual duties and motivates us to act morally with the weak force of good reasons. However, this cognitivism is aimed at the insight of individuals and does not foster any impulse towards solidary, that is, towards morally guided, collective action. To be sure, this morality also involves a practice in which children develop a moral consciousness, normally in the context of their families and peer groups. A result of successful moral socialization, however, is that the adult person relies primarily on her own judgment and conscience. Secular morality is not inherently embedded in communal practices. Religious consciousness, by contrast, preserves an essential connection to the ongoing practice of life within a community and, in the case of the major world religions, to the observances of united global communities of all of the faithful. The religious consciousness of the individual can derive stronger impulses towards action in solidarity, even from a purely moral point of view, from this universalistic communitarianism. Whether this is still the case today I leave to one side.

It may be of interest for the question of who is missing what that Kant felt it to be a major deficiency that practical reason is unable to justify the realization of collective goals based on solidarity or the cooperative averting of collective dangers as convincingly and effectively as the individual observance of moral duties. He regarded the philosophical assimilation of religious traditions as the correct way to make good this deficiency. In a commentary on the translation of the Christian notion of *fides* into morally motivated rational belief, he defends his procedure as follows: "[T]hat is not the only case where this wonderful religion in the great simplicity of its expression has enriched morality with far more determinate and pure concepts than morality itself could previously supply, but which, once they exist, are freely approved by reason and assumed as ones that it could have arrived at" (*Critique of the Power of Judgement*, 5: 472, p. 336, n.). However, to this Kant adds an additional relative clause: "... (concepts) which it (reason) could and should have introduced

75

by itself." But can't philosophy arrive at the counterfactual conviction that it could have discovered them itself only retrospectively, after it has combed the concepts from foreign beaches?

This is why I think it makes sense to re-examine the relation between philosophy and religion from the perspective of the Axial Age. However, whether a different perspective on the genealogy of reason can enable post-metaphysical thinking to deal with the problem specified by Kant – or even lead us to a better understanding of the diagnosis of the breakdown of solidarity – is a question which I have deliberately left open.

(2) Michael Reder is rightly dissatisfied with a functionalist conception of religion which, although it has a legitimate place in political science and sociology, is insufficient in the context of a philosophical self-reflection on the relation between faith and knowledge. This lack of clarity can be dispelled by reflecting on the standpoint from which one speaks in each case. Functionalist approaches to religion have their place even in the context of a normative political theory, for here one argues from the perspective of the need for legitimation of the constitutional state. From this perspective, religious communities and Churches can play an active role in the political arena and pursue their own agenda insofar as they understand themselves as communities of interpretation and relinquish ecclesiastical authority – that is, insofar as they offer only arguments which are aimed at believers in their role as citizens. This is in the interest of democratic communities which want to avoid overhastily cutting themselves off from resources of meaning, solidarity, and justice which are becoming depleted. The recommendation to handle religious traditions with care can also be justified in functional terms from the perspective of social theory. In both cases it is a matter of counterbalancing functional deficits (given the reality of a "modernization spinning out of control"). However, the assumed potential of buried or untapped

semantic resources, which are for the present inaccessible to secular reason, appears in a completely different light from the performative perspective of a self-reflection of postmetaphysical thinking. For a philosophy which relates to religion as a contemporary intellectual formation enters into a dialogue with it instead of talking about it. The second-person stance of a philosophy which adopts a stance towards religion which is at once agnostic and willing to learn cannot be reconciled with the instrumental stance towards the target of a hostile takeover.

A point of disagreement with Michael Reder concerns how "religion" should be understood in this context. For an agnostic person who is concerned with the self-understanding of postmetaphysical thinking and not with the issue of the *proprium* of faith in the philosophy of religion, the word "religion" (here one could think of Karl Barth) cannot have the same meaning as for the person of faith. Following Max Weber, though *not* for sociological reasons, I draw upon the heritage of those "strong" traditions whose origin can be traced back to the Axial Age and which have retained their power to shape civilization, into the very definitional conflicts of a multicultural world society, until the present day. Against this, Reder insists that we must take account of the "diversity of religious–cultural hybrid forms." I am not altogether sure what he means by this. However, his objection prompts me to offer a precautionary explanation of my narrow focus on the major world religions.

On the one hand, anyone who is interested in the present constellation of postmetaphysical thinking, religion, and science must examine the genealogy of the peculiar affinity between metaphysics and the coeval East Asian traditions of Hinduism, Confucianism, and, above all, Buddhism. On the other hand, an unexhausted semantic potential, assuming that such exists, can be found only in traditions which, although their mythical kernel was transformed into a thinking of transcendence through the cognitive advance of the Axial Age, nevertheless have not

77

yet completely dissolved in the relentless acceleration of modern conditions of life. The Californian syncretism of pseudoscientific and esoteric doctrines and religious fundamentalism are thoroughly modern phenomena which may even express social pathologies of modernity, but which certainly do not offer any resistance to them. The missionary successes of a literal, but liturgically extravagant spiritualism are certainly also interesting from sociological points of view. However, I cannot see what importance religious movements which cut themselves off from the cognitive achievements of modernity could have for the secular self-understanding of modernity.

My, if you will, narcissistically limited focus on the question of the "self-assertion of reason" (Kant) accounts for my preference for traditions which, like Christianity and Buddhism, have achieved a high level of internal rationalization in the course of their dogmatic elaboration. For they have thereby also inadvertently laid the groundwork for a possible dissociation of semantic contents from the premises of their respective revealed truths. Already respect for this rational potential of human experiences requires us to distinguish religious traditions from other worldviews and ethical plans of life. Of course, there is a certain functional equivalence between the paths to salvation of a religion which, for example, enjoins us to emulate Christ, and the various secular conceptions of a good or not misspent life which are geared "to us" or "to me." However, with the individualization of our self-interpretive discourses, these ethical conceptions underwent a pronounced differentiation, multiplication, and subjectivization. They attain a comparable level of articulation to the doctrines of salvation of the major religions only in the classical wisdom teachings transmitted by philosophy. Of course, these argumentatively articulated existential orientations have also lost their claim to universality in the light of the pluralism of worldviews. They appeal to some people more than to others and – in contrast to conceptions of justice which are justified in universalistic terms, that is, which are directed "to all" and "to everyone equally" – no longer claim to be collectively binding.

Religions, by contrast, raise a strict claim to truth not only for their moral principles but also for their theologically or cosmologically justified paths to salvation. They are *not* reducible to "ethical" worldviews. After all, only this circumstance gives rise to the political challenge of religious pluralism, which found an answer in the modern conception of toleration – that is, in a conception which allows the religious communities to recognize one another while nevertheless upholding their respective exclusive claims to truth (Forst 2003). I have no idea how one could convince the citizens of a secular state of this conception without separating rational morality strictly from ethical and religious convictions.

(3) I find Friedo Ricken's reflections so convincing that I can confine myself to a couple of remarks. Because I share his respect for Kant's critique of metaphysics (Ricken 2003, pp. 193–232), our agreement also extends to his critical engagement with the theological content of the Pope's Regensburg address. Regarding Kant's philosophy of religion, we differ only in our assessments of the systematic robustness of its central argument (Habermas 2008, pp. 209–47). Important here is the reference to the different roles which philosophical "translations" of religious contents have played, and can still play, in the history of theology and philosophy.

From its beginnings and into the early modern period, Christian theology drew upon the conceptual apparatus of Greek metaphysics to make explicit the contents of the faith and to subject them to discursive treatment. This labor of dogmatization must not destroy the core of faith and is subject to the reservation that the communities must be able to recognize their own faith in the theological doctrines. Here the internal rationalization of the transmitted doctrines serves the need to justify a religion to itself and to the world. Something completely different is meant when secular reason tries to use the means of postmetaphysical thinking to assimilate contents from the Christian tradition in accordance with its own standards. In this way, part of the Christian heritage is transposed into the horizon of discourses of justification which no longer measure themselves against the authority of the lived faith but against the standards of the relevant valid factual knowledge. Since Hegel and the rise of historical thinking, philosophy has discovered this religious heritage within itself. Philosophical concepts such as those of the person, freedom, and individuation, history and emancipation, community and solidarity, are infused with experiences and connotations which stem from the biblical teaching and its tradition. Since that time, this process of the assimilation of unexhausted contents has been continued by religious authors from Kierkegaard to Bloch and Benjamin, Lévinas and Derrida. What counts on the philosophical side is the persuasiveness which philosophical translations acquire for the secular environment.

(4) Josef Schmidt recognizes and accepts the self-referential character of the critical question about reason that concerns me here: "Secular reason must face the question of where it has drawn its own rational boundaries too hastily, so that the latter do not match its real scope." In spite of Hegel's famous critique of the Kantian demarcations, Kant's question concerning the self-understanding of a self-critical reason remains valid. Depending on the arguments in question, this question repeatedly arises as one concerning the correct kind of self-limitation. A finite reason which is embodied in historical time and in the social space of cultural forms of life cannot determine these limits at its own discretion. It must understand itself from out of a constellation as a cognitive undertaking which finds itself in predefined relations to science and religion. Secular reason can develop such a self-understanding without prejudice to its autonomy even if, in assimilating religion, it does treat it as an inferior intellectual formation.

Then, however, it may not accept the predefined constellation as a mere fact (as an "occurrence" [*Ereignis*]), but
must seek to understand it as the result of a learning
process.

The humanist self-confidence of a philosophical
reason which thinks that it is capable of determining
what is true and false in the "truths" handed down by
religion has in the meantime – as a result of the catastro-
phes of the twentieth century – been shaken not only in
a historical-political sense. Karl Jaspers and John Rawls
concluded in different ways that these traditions should
be treated in a rigorously agnostic manner, though one
which is anxious to understand and is even willing to learn.
Yet both of them pay a high price – too high a price – for
reserving judgment (while insisting on a strict demarca-
tion). Jaspers assimilates philosophical knowledge to
the mode of revealed faith, whereas Rawls renounces
the claim to truth of a practical reason decoupled from
worldviews.

Josef Schmidt correctly emphasizes that with the "universally binding reference to truth . . . the horizon of an
inclusive community" opens up; to this communication
community belong all those who even implicitly understand what we mean when we say that something is the
case or that an injunction is morally binding. In every
discursive exchange a reason operates which compels the
participants to make idealizing presuppositions – for
example, to presuppose that competing claims to truth
and rightness can be examined in the medium of free-
floating reasons and information and that they can be
criticized or redeemed on the basis of rationally motivated
"yes" or "no" stances. Such communicative presuppositions are ineluctable for anyone who so much as engages
in discourse. Sober postmetaphysical thinking, however,
identifies in this only the "unconditionality" of a factually
unavoidable claim of reason.

The theologian or the metaphysician will see in this
unconditionality a connection to the idea of God or of an

absolute origin: "As regards the approach to the discussion of the idea of God, what is specific to the concept of God will be rationally represented to faith in the unavoidable reflexive circle of reason." Now, the agnostic person can and must leave these more far-reaching features alone insofar as she encounters in her counterpart a receptiveness to the inherent logic and authority of the sciences and to the autonomous justification of morality and law. A direct link must not be permitted between the universal morality and the respective particular worldviews, "such that someone could say, for example, 'since I do not share such and such a comprehensive view, the requirements of morality do not hold for me either'."

On the other hand, the same forms of reflection which we owe to the scientific-technical, procedural-legal, and social achievements of modernity can also lead us into the dead end of a dialectic of enlightenment. The encounter with theology can remind a self-forgetful, secular reason of its distant origins in the revolution in worldviews of the Axial Age. Since the Judeo-Christian and Arabian traditions are no less a part of the inheritance of postmetaphysical thinking than Greek metaphysics, biblical motifs can remind us, for example, of dimensions of a reasonable personal self-understanding which have been abandoned too hastily.

My conversational partners provide examples of this. Friedo Ricken mentions an interpretation of human freedom rooted in the theology of creation which can find a reasonable response in secular thought when it is a matter of clarifying the limits of human self-objectification and self-manipulation. Another example is the First Commandment, which Josef Schmidt understands in the sense of enabling human beings to transcend everything within the world.[1] Philosophy, too, must hold fast to this intuition, though in its own way, if the difference

---

[1] "The worship of the one God liberates human beings from all possible idols and earthly powers."

between facticity and validity is not to be leveled in a contextualist manner. We can only "master" a language of whose *logos* we heed; at the same time, this *logos* liberates us from the subjection to the immediacy of events and occurrences in the world, because we gain intentional distance from the world as a whole through intersubjective communication about something in the world.

References

Anacker, Ulrich (1974). "Vernunft." In *Handbuch philoso-phischer Grundbegriffe*, Vol. 6, ed. Hermann Krings (Munich: Kösel), pp. 1597–1612.

Arens, Edmund (ed.) (1989). *Habermas und die Theologie: Beiträge zur theologischen Rezeption, Diskussion und Kritik der Theorie kommunikativen Handelns*. Düsseldorf: Patmos.

Benedict XVI. (2006). "Faith, Reason and the University: Memories and Reflections." Address delivered at the University of Regensburg on Tuesday, September 12, 2006 (http://www.vatican.va/holy_father/benedict_xvi/speeches/2006/september/documents/hf_ben-xvi_spe_20060912_university-regensburg_en.html) (accessed March 2009).

Bloch, Ernst (1964). "Something's Missing: A Discussion between Ernst Bloch and Theodor W. Adorno on the Contradictions of Utopian Longing." In Bloch, *The Utopian Function of Art and Literature*, trans. Jack Zipes and Frank Mecklenburg (Cambridge, Mass.: MIT Press, 1989), pp. 1–17.

Comte, Auguste (1997). *Auguste Comte and Positivism: The Essential Writings*. Ed. Gertrade Larzer. Piscataway, NJ: Transaction.

Cooke, Maeve (2007). "Säkulare Übersetzung oder post-säkulare Argumentation? Habermas über Religion in der demokratischen Öffentlichkeit." In *Glauben und Wissen: Ein Symposium mit Jürgen Habermas über Religion*, eds Rudolf Langthaler and Herta Nagl-Docekal (Vienna: Oldenbourg, Berlin: Akademie), pp. 341–64.

84

Danz, Christian (2007). "Religion zwischen Aneignung und Kritik. Überlegungen zur Religionstheorie von Jürgen Habermas." In *Glauben und Wissen: Ein Symposium mit Jürgen Habermas über Religion*, eds Rudolf Langthaler and Herta Nagl-Docekal (Vienna: Oldenbourg, Berlin: Akademie), pp. 9–31.

Derrida, Jacques, and Vattimo, Gianni (eds) (1998). *Religion*. Stanford, Ca.: Stanford University Press.

Ebeling, Hans (1990). *Neue Subjektivität: Die Selbstbehauptung der Vernunft*. Würzburg: Königshausen and Neumann.

Eckert, Michael (1987). *Gott, Glauben und Wissen: F. D. Schleiermachers Philosophische Theologie*. Berlin and New York: W. de Gruyter.

Forst, Rainer (2003). *Toleranz im Konflikt: Geschichte, Gehalt und Gegenwart eines umstrittenen Begriffs*. Frankfurt am Main: Suhrkamp.

Frank, Manfred (1977). "Einleitung." In *Hermeneutik und Kritik: Mit einem Anhang sprachphilosophischer Texte Schleiermachers*, ed. Manfred Frank (Frankfurt am Main: Suhrkamp), pp. 7–67.

Graf, Friedrich Wilhelm (2004). *Die Wiederkehr der Götter: Religion in der modernen Kultur*. Munich: Beck.

Habermas, Jürgen (1978). *Politik, Kunst, Religion: Essays über zeitgenössische Philosophen*. Stuttgart: Reclam.

– (1984, 1987). *The Theory of Communicative Action*. 2 vols. Trans. Thomas McCarthy. Boston: Beacon.

– (1991a). *Moral Consciousness and Communicative Action*. Trans. Christian Lenhardt and Shierry Weber Nicholsen. Cambridge, Mass.: MIT Press.

– (1991b). "Philosophy as Stand-in and Interpreter." In Habermas, *Moral Consciousness and Communicative Action*, pp. 1–20.

– (1993). *Justification and Application: Remarks on Discourse Ethics*. Trans. Ciaran Cronin. Cambridge, Mass.: MIT Press.

– (2001). *On the Pragmatics of Social Interaction*. Trans. Barbara Fultner. Cambridge, Mass.: MIT Press.

– (2003). "Faith and Knowledge." In Habermas, *The Future of Human Nature*, trans. William Rehg, Max Pensky, and Hella Beister (Cambridge: Polity), pp. 101–15.

– (2007a). "Ein Bewusstsein von dem, was fehlt. Über Glauben und Wissen und den Defaitismus der modernen Vernunft." In

Neue Zürcher Zeitung, February 10, 2007 (http://www.nzz.
ch/2007/02/10/li/articleEVB7X.html) (accessed March
2009).
– (2007b). "Replik auf Einwände, Reaktion auf Anregungen."
In *Glauben und Wissen: Ein Symposium mit Jürgen Habermas
über Religion*, eds Rudolf Langthaler and Herta Nagl-Docekal
(Vienna: Oldenbourg, Berlin: Akademie), pp. 366–414.
– (2008). *Between Naturalism and Religion*. Trans. Ciaran
Cronin. Cambridge: Polity.
Haunhorst, Benno (2000). "Katholizismus und Sozialdemokra-
tie." In *Religion ist keine Privatsache*, ed. Wolfgang Thierse
(Düsseldorf: Patmos), pp. 16–28.
Inthorn, Julia, and Reder, Michael (2005). *Philosophie und
Mathematik bei Cusanus: Eine Verhältnisbestimmung von
dialektischem und binärem Denken*. Trier: Paulinus.
Joas, Hans (2008). *Do We Need Religion? On the Experience of
Self Transcendence*. Trans. Alex Skinner. Boulder, Co.: Para-
digm Publishers.
Kant, Immanuel (1998a). *Religion within the Boundaries of
Mere Reason and Other Writings*. Ed. and trans. Allen Wood
and George di Giovanni. Cambridge: Cambridge University
Press.
– (1998b). *Critique of Pure Reason*. Ed. and trans. Paul Guyer
and Allen Wood. Cambridge: Cambridge University Press.
– (2000). *Critique of the Power of Judgement*. Ed. Paul Guyer.
Trans. Paul Guyer and Eric Matthews. Cambridge: Cam-
bridge University Press.
Langthaler, Rudolf and Nagl-Docekal, Herta (eds) (2007).
*Glauben und Wissen: Ein Symposium mit Jürgen Habermas
über Religion*. Vienna: Oldenbourg, Berlin: Akademie.
Maly, Sebastian (2005). "Die Rolle der Religion in der postsäkularen Gesellschaft: Zur Religionsphilosophie von Jürgen
Habermas." *Theologie und Philosophie* 80: 546–65.
Marcuse, Herbert (1971). "The Concept of Negation in the
Dialectic." *Telos* 8: 130–2.
Metz, Johann Baptist (2006). *Memoria passionis: Ein provozie-
rendes Gedächtnis in pluraler Gesellschaft*. Freiburg im Breis-
gau, Basel, Vienna: Herder.
Müller, Johannes (2007). "Religionen – Quelle von Gewalt
oder Anwalt der Menschen? Überlegungen zu den Ursachen
der Ambivalenz von Religionen." In *Religionen und Global-*

isierung, eds Johannes Müller, Michael Reder and Tobias Karcher (Stuttgart: Kohlhammer), pp. 119–37.)

Ratzinger, Joseph (1982). *Zeitfragen und christlicher Glaube: Acht Predigten aus den Münchner Jahren.* Würzburg: Naumann.

— (2008). *Church, Ecumenism, and Politics: New Endeavors in Ecclesiology.* Trans. Michael J. Miller, et al. San Francisco: Ignatius Press.

Reder, Michael (2006). *Global Governance: Philosophische Modelle von Weltpolitik.* Darmstadt: Wissenschaftliches Buchgesellschaft.

Ricken, Friedo (2003). *Religionsphilosophie.* Stuttgart: Kohlhammer.

Rorty, Richard, and Vattimo, Gianni (2005). *The Future of Religion.* Ed. Santiago Zabala. New York: Columbia University Press.

Schmidt, Thomas M. (2007). "Religiöser Diskurs und diskursive Religion in der postsäkularen Gesellschaft." In *Glauben und Wissen: Ein Symposium mit Jürgen Habermas über Religion*, eds Rudolf Langthaler and Herta Nagl-Docekal (Vienna: Oldenbourg, Berlin: Akademie), pp. 322–340.

Spinoza, Baruch (2007). *Theological–Political Treatise,* eds Jonathan Israel and Michael Silverthorne. Trans. Michael Silverthorne. Cambridge: Cambridge University Press.

Suárez, Francisco (2002) *Abhandlung über die Gesetze und Gott den Gesetzgeber. Bk. I and II.* Trans. and ed. Norbert Brieskorn. Freiburg im Breisgau and Berlin: Haufe-Mediengruppe.

Thierse, Wolfgang (ed.) (2000). *Religion ist keine Privatsache.* Düsseldorf: Patmos.

Werbick, Jürgen (2000). "'Religion ist keine Privatsache!' Theologische Einwände gegen eine politisch allzu bequeme Floskel." In *Religion ist keine Privatsache,* ed. Wolfgang Thierse (Düsseldorf: Patmos), pp. 90–105.